Talking With God

Daily Readings Through the Psalms

TODAY IN THE WORD
Ryan Cook

MOODY PUBLISHERS
CHICAGO

© 2025 by
TODAY IN THE WORD

All rights reserved. No part of this book may be reproduced in any form without permission in writing from the publisher, except in the case of brief quotations embodied in critical articles or reviews.

All Scripture quotations, unless otherwise indicated, are taken from the Holy Bible, New International Version®, NIV®. Copyright ©1973, 1978, 1984, 2011 by Biblica, Inc.™ Used by permission of Zondervan. All rights reserved worldwide. www.zondervan.com The "NIV" and "New International Version" are trademarks registered in the United States Patent and Trademark Office by Biblica, Inc.™

Scripture quotations marked (ESV) are from the ESV® Bible (The Holy Bible, English Standard Version®), © 2001 by Crossway, a publishing ministry of Good News Publishers. Used by permission. All rights reserved. The ESV text may not be quoted in any publication made available to the public by a Creative Commons license. The ESV may not be translated in whole or in part into any other language.

Edited by Jamie Janosz, Elena Mafter, and Avrie Roberts
Interior design: Graham Terry
Cover design: Darren Welch
Cover photo of mountains copyright © 2024 by Titov Dmtriy/Shutterstock (1104650822). All rights reserved.

ISBN 978-0-8024-3611-5

Originally delivered by fleets of horse-drawn wagons, the affordable paperbacks from D. L. Moody's publishing house resourced the church and served everyday people. Now, after more than 125 years of publishing and ministry, Moody Publishers' mission remains the same—even if our delivery systems have changed a bit. For more information on other books (and resources) created from a biblical perspective, go to www.moodypublishers.com or write to:

Moody Publishers
820 N. LaSalle Boulevard
Chicago, IL 60610

1 3 5 7 9 10 8 6 4 2

Printed in the United States of America

To the faithful readers of *Today in the Word*, who join us every day to open and learn from God's Word.

Table of Contents

Foreword		11
Introduction		15
BOOK 1	**(Psalms 1–41)**	**21**
Psalm 1	Delight in God's Word	23
Psalm 2	Delight in God's King	25
Psalm 3	The Lies of the Enemy	27
Psalm 4	Turn Your Eyes upon Yahweh	29
Psalm 5	Waiting on God	31
Psalm 6	Not Too Proud to Beg	33
Psalm 7	God of Justice	35
Psalm 8	God of Wonders	37
Psalm 9	The ABCs of Praise and Lament: Part 1	39
Psalm 10	The ABCs of Praise and Lament: Part 2	41
Psalm 11	Flight or Faith	43
Psalm 12	Surrounded by Lies	45
Psalm 13	Lament as Grief	47
Psalm 14	Practical Atheism	49
Psalm 15	Invitation to Worship	51
Psalm 16	Count Your Blessings	53
Psalm 17	Your Kingdom Come	55
Psalm 18	Rescued at Last	57
Psalm 19	Speaking of His Wonder	59
Psalm 20	God Hears My Cry	61
Psalm 21	A Victory Song	63
Psalm 22	From Despair to Hope	65
Psalm 23	The Good Shepherd	67
Psalm 24	The Owner of All	69
Psalm 25	In God We Trust	71
Psalm 26	What Do You Love?	73
Psalm 27	The One Thing	75
Psalm 28	Hear My Cry	77

Psalm 29	The Lord Is King	79
Psalm 30	Praise Is Life	81
Psalm 31	Our Refuge	83
Psalm 32	The Blessed One	85
Psalm 33	A Singing Faith	87
Psalm 34	Taste and See	89
Psalm 35	God of Justice	91
Psalm 36	Be Not Proud	93
Psalm 37	Finding Significance	95
Psalm 38	Suffering and Sin	97
Psalm 39	Life Is Short	99
Psalm 40	Giving Thanks	101
Psalm 41	How to Be Like God	103
BOOK 2	**(Psalms 42–72)**	**105**
Psalm 42	Longing for God	107
Psalm 43	Hope in Lament	109
Psalm 44	Awake, Lord!	111
Psalm 45	Future Hope	113
Psalm 46	A Mighty Fortress	115
Psalm 47	Clap Your Hands	117
Psalm 48	Great Is Your Faithfulness	119
Psalm 49	Wealth and God	121
Psalm 50	Wrong Motives	123
Psalm 51	True Repentance	125
Psalm 52	Destructive Words	127
Psalm 53	All Have Sinned	129
Psalm 54	Crying for Help	131
Psalm 55	When Betrayed	133
Psalm 56	When I Fear	135
Psalm 57	Safe with You	137
Psalm 58	Longing for Justice	139
Psalm 59	A Broken World	141
Psalm 60	The Promises of God	143
Psalm 61	Hear My Cry	145

Psalm 62	Rest in God	147
Psalm 63	Better than Life	149
Psalm 64	The Hope of the Righteous	151
Psalm 65	Praise God	153
Psalm 66	Come and See!	155
Psalm 67	Praying for Blessing	157
Psalm 68	Names of God	159
Psalm 69	Save Me, God	161
Psalm 70	Saving Help	163
Psalm 71	I Will Praise You	165
Psalm 72	Your Kingdom Come	167
BOOK 3	**(Psalms 73–89)**	**169**
Psalm 73	A Vision of God	171
Psalm 74	Rise Up, O God!	173
Psalm 75	The Cup of God's Wrath	175
Psalm 76	The Power of God	177
Psalm 77	Our Waymaker	179
Psalm 78	Knowing God	181
Psalm 79	Where Is God?	183
Psalm 80	Revive Us, O God!	185
Psalm 81	True Worship	187
Psalm 82	God of Justice	189
Psalm 83	Grace in Judgment	191
Psalm 84	Longing for God	193
Psalm 85	Justice and Forgiveness	195
Psalm 86	An Anchor for the Soul	197
Psalm 87	The God of Zion and the God of the Nations	199
Psalm 88	Darkness Is My Closest Friend	201
Psalm 89	Remember God's Promises	203
BOOK 4	**(Psalms 90–106)**	**205**
Psalm 90	Life and Death	207
Psalm 91	Safely Home	209
Psalm 92	Made to Worship	211
Psalm 93	Who's in Charge?	213

Psalm 94	Judge of All	215
Psalm 95	Wholehearted Worship	217
Psalm 96	Sing to the Lord!	219
Psalm 97	God Is King	221
Psalm 98	Joy to the World	223
Psalm 99	A Just and Merciful God	225
Psalm 100	Our True Identity	227
Psalm 101	Holy Worship	229
Psalm 102	Clinging to God	231
Psalm 103	Amazing Grace	233
Psalm 104	This Is My Father's World	235
Psalm 105	Family History	237
Psalm 106	O God, Our Help in Ages Past	239
BOOK 5	**(Psalms 107–150)**	**241**
Psalm 107	Unfailing Love	243
Psalm 108	Help Me, God!	245
Psalm 109	Living in an Unjust World	247
Psalm 110	The Coming Messiah	249
Psalm 111	The Alphabet of Praise	251
Psalm 112	A Portrait of Faith	253
Psalm 113	Who Is Like the Lord?	255
Psalm 114	We Remember	257
Psalm 115	Trust in the Lord!	259
Psalm 116	Can I Get a Witness?	261
Psalm 117	Let the Nations Rejoice!	263
Psalm 118	He Is God!	265
Psalm 119: 1–88	Precious Words	267
Psalm 119: 89–176	Words of Life	269
Psalm 120	Longing for Peace	271
Psalm 121	Looking for Help	273
Psalm 122	City of Peace	275

Psalm 123	Lift Up My Eyes	277
Psalm 124	Seeing God in Suffering	279
Psalm 125	Joyfully Secure	281
Psalm 126	Filled with Joy	283
Psalm 127	Work and Rest	285
Psalm 128	Blessing and Prosperity	287
Psalm 129	Persevering in Pain	289
Psalm 130	Hope in Suffering	291
Psalm 131	Content in God	293
Psalm 132	Two Commitments	295
Psalm 133	Life Together	297
Psalm 134	Circle of Blessing	299
Psalm 135	Who Do You Worship?	301
Psalm 136	Loved by God	303
Psalm 137	We Sat and Wept	305
Psalm 138	Longing for the Past	307
Psalm 139	God with Us	309
Psalm 140	God of Justice	311
Psalm 141	Fixed on You	313
Psalm 142	Speak Up!	315
Psalm 143	Hear My Prayer!	317
Psalm 144	A New Song	319
Psalm 145	Great Is the Lord	321
Psalm 146	As Long as I Live	323
Psalm 147	Grateful Praise	325
Psalm 148	Praise the Lord!	327
Psalm 149	Fight Song	329
Psalm 150	Hallelujah!	331

| About the Authors | 333 |
| Notes | 335 |

Foreword

Whether you are opening the Bible for the very first time or are a Christ follower who has read the Scriptures many times over, it is not surprising that we return to the Psalms again and again. Why? It is not just because this book is easy to find, right in the center of our Bibles. I think it is because in the Psalms we find raw, honest, heartfelt communication with God.

If you've ever struggled to talk to God, I believe this book will help and encourage you in that conversation. In the Psalms, we learn how to talk with God in a way that is authentic and real. David and the other authors of the Psalms show us how we can stay connected with God during good times and bad. They praise God for His help in the past and cry out with frustration at the grave injustices in their lives. They speak of desperate loneliness and heart-wrenching grief. They express joy during times of victory and wonder at God's breathtaking creation. From sorrow to joy, the entire range of human emotion is on display. The Psalms reflect who we are. And as we read this book, it connects us to God.

Although written centuries ago, the Psalms never feel outdated. The words prayed by the psalmists so many centuries ago speak directly to our current situations and help us navigate our modern world. They point us back to God when our relationship with Him feels fractured or dulled, when we seem to have lost our way.

As a pastor for many years, many people have asked me how to pray. They say, "How can I pray in a way that matters?" Some were taught to pray as a child, memorizing words to repeat again and again. Others have recited prayers in church, even as an adult, but somehow it just didn't connect with what was on their heart and mind. So they set prayer aside, or leave it to the professionals.

But when our world turns upside down, when life presses in and we find ourselves bending under the struggles, we find that we need to pray. And in those times, I believe you will find that the Psalms will guide you. Here you will find the words to express the deepest needs in your heart.

Reading the Psalms takes the focus off ourselves and puts it on God. We learn to praise even when the path before us seems cloudy. As we walk through the Psalms, we discover that praise is closer than we think. Psalm 118:1 helps us find our praise . . . right in the neighborhood of thanksgiving. "Give thanks to the LORD, for he is good; his love endures forever."

In the Psalms, we are reminded how to praise, a language naturally spoken by children of God. When we find ourselves speaking the language of complaining or ingratitude, we are not speaking our native language. True praise can be possible even when we don't feel good about the world in which we live.

Psalm 7:17 is just one reminder of why we praise, "I will give thanks to the LORD because of his righteousness." The One who orchestrates the destiny of men and who laid a foundation for all creation, is intrinsically good. Our God who has existed for all eternity—who is all knowing, all powerful, ever present in every time and space—in His very nature is good!

These studies were originally written for *Today in the Word*, a daily devotional published by Moody Bible Institute since 1988 and now read by more than one million people. This series of devotionals on the Psalms, authored by Moody professor Dr. Ryan Cook, has been a reader favorite for good reason.

In this book, you are invited to read through the Psalms in their entirety. You might decide to read it straight through as one book or reflect on one psalm a day. You can study it alone or with a group. But no matter how you engage with it, I know you will be blessed as you spend time in God's Word.

You will be reminded again and again of God's love and care for you. Thirty-six times in the Psalms we are reassured that "[God's] love endures forever." God's love will never change; it is constant. We don't have a God who one day is good and the other day bad. We serve a God whose very nature is good—every good and perfect gift comes directly from Him. We know that His love will never end.

Friend, I do not know what your circumstances look like right now. Your health may not be great. Your finances may not be in the top condition. But I know that the nature of God will never change. I encourage you, no matter what your situation, to read through one psalm a day, to be reminded of who God is and of how much He cares for you. It is better than your morning cup of coffee. It is better than your daily vitamin.

It is our prayer that God will meet you here, in the pages of His Word. That this study of the Psalms will refresh and reenergize your prayer life. That you will discover for the first time, or be reminded again, that God goes before you and beside you. We can talk to Him anywhere, at any time, and about anything. How wonderful to have a God who cares so deeply and intimately for us.

Dr. Mark Jobe
President, Moody Bible Institute

Introduction

My earliest memory of the book of Psalms is from my kindergarten Bible class. Over the course of a few weeks, our teacher Mrs. Thornman led us in memorizing Psalm 23 in the beautiful language of the King James Version. My understanding of God as a young child was deeply shaped by the central image of the psalm, "The LORD is my shepherd" (Ps. 23:1). I envisioned God as a caring and protective presence in my life.

Many years later, as a pastor, I began reading from the early church fathers for twenty minutes a day. For over a year, I read different books by the north African bishop Augustine. About halfway through that year, it struck me how often Augustine quoted from or used the language of the Psalms. I decided to do a little research. I discovered that over the course of thirty years of his life, Augustine worked on a commentary on the Psalms that fills six volumes in English translation.[1] In addition to that massive work, Augustine either quotes from or clearly alludes to the Psalms over 10,000 times in his other writing.[2] The way he was saturated in the language of the Psalms was fascinating to me. I wondered, *What would it look like for someone to know the Psalms so well that your language and theology were shaped by them?* Perhaps the Psalms are included in the Bible to do just that.

When I later went on to earn a PhD in Biblical Studies, my dissertation was focused on Psalms interpretation. So for the last decade and a half, the Psalms have been a constant companion in my devotional life, in the seminary classroom, and in my academic work.

One of the purposes of the book of Psalms is that it provides us with examples of how to speak with God in just about every situation that life can throw at us. Of course, the Psalms do far more than that. They teach profound truths about God's nature and character, and they prophesy about the coming Messiah. But one of their most important functions is to give us language that we can imitate in our own life with God. As a young child learns to speak their native language, we learn appropriate ways of addressing God.

How did you learn to speak your native language? Did someone sit you down one day and teach you the grammar, syntax, and vocabulary of the language? Of course not! Can you imagine trying to get a two-year-old to sit still for more than fifteen seconds? But by the time you entered school at age four or five, you already had a good grasp of the language. How did that come about? You learned by listening to and imitating those around you. From real life experience with your family, you picked up on not just the meaning of words but on what kind of speech was appropriate in different situations. You probably learned to not call your parents by their first names. You learned the right way to ask for things and to express your needs and wants.

This book is a devotional guide to the Psalms. My hope is that these devotional reflections will help you engage more deeply in the book of Psalms. To that end, I would like to offer a few tips for reading the Psalms as you work through this book. First, it is important to recognize that the Psalms are poetry. Poetry is not meant to be read quickly. The language is carefully selected, and the authors use vivid images and metaphors. So, when you read the Psalms, don't be in a hurry. Slow down and savor the feel and flow of the text. Meditate on the images used by the authors. For example, consider Psalm 1:3,

Introduction

> That person is like a tree planted by streams of water,
> which yields its fruit in season
> And whose leaf does not wither—
> Whatever they do prospers.

The righteous person here is compared to a flourishing tree. What is the significance of that comparison? Imagine a tree planted in rich, well-watered soil. A tree with strong roots will endure. It will last for generations. Because it is richly nourished, the tree will bless others. But this not just any tree, it's a fruit tree! Many people will be nourished and refreshed by its produce. The tree is a source of life and blessing to others. All of this meaning, and more, is packed into this image. The image of the stable, enduring, life-giving tree of the righteous is contrasted in the psalm with the wicked. The wicked are depicted as "chaff that the wind blows away" (v. 4). Chaff is not enduring, not fruitful, and is of no use to anyone. It also does not last long. One brief gust of wind and the chaff disappears. There is a reason why the psalmist uses metaphors like this to communicate truth about the righteous and the wicked. These metaphors strike our imagination and get under our skin in a way that normal language does not.

The Psalms were originally written in Hebrew. Hebrew poetry works a bit differently than most poetry in English. Instead of a rhyming scheme or syllable count, Hebrew poems are structured through thought rhymes or parallelism. Two, or sometimes three, lines will work together to produce one unit of thought. For example, consider Psalm 6:2,

> Have mercy on me, LORD, for I am faint;
> heal me, LORD, for my bones are in agony

These two lines are clearly parallel. The second line sharpens or carries forward the meaning in the first line. In the first line, David says, "Have mercy on me, LORD, for I am faint." What does he mean by that? How does he want to see God's mercy in his life? The second line carries the thought forward and makes the request more specific, "Heal me, LORD, for my bones are in agony." Now we understand that David is suffering from physical distress. The plea to "heal me!" is much more specific than "have mercy on me." Also, "my bones are in agony" is a more vivid and memorable image than "I am faint." The psalmists will often state the general theme in the first line, then sharpen it in the second line. Simply understanding this dynamic will help you read the Psalms more attentively and accurately.

Finally, I would encourage you to pray through the Psalms as you read them. Make the Psalms part of your relationship with God. This may seem awkward at first, especially with psalms of lament. I have often had students ask me how they could pray a lament if they were not personally suffering. To some, it feels a bit dishonest to cry out, "LORD, how many are my foes! How many rise up against me!" (Ps. 3:1), when there is not an enemy in sight in their own life. There are a couple of ways to think about this. First, we can pray this language so that we have words and prayers to use when we do face persecution or suffering. This language will help us be equipped in our relationship with God even for circumstances we have not experienced yet. Second, we can pray these Psalms on behalf of others in the world who are suffering and being persecuted. One Psalms scholar describes this dynamic in this way:

> Every time a person recites the complaints, he or she vicariously becomes one who faces injustice, who hungers, is sick

and frightened. It is as if God does not narrow the focus to one particular case, but sees the whole drama of humanity, yesterday and today. The psalms open our ears, eyes, and hearts to human cries beyond us. Insofar as we accept this way of reciting them, the cry of the oppressed invades our space, occupies our prayer, and grounds our daily troubles in the misfortune of humanity. The prison, hospital, war zone, and slum invades our . . . church . . . and there is an exchange. Those for whom we pray, whose voice becomes ours, enlarge our hearts and transform us by their suffering. To pray and say "I" in the place of persons who are most tested is an invitation to sympathize with them.[3]

This articulates powerfully the importance of including laments both in our personal worship and in the corporate worship of the church. As long as believers regularly pray the Psalms, the weak, needy, and oppressed will have a voice. It is one way we can bear one another's burdens.

As I have prayed, studied, and taught the Psalms, I am continually struck by the psalmists' honesty with God, the careful artistry of their poems, and how they shape their relationship with God in joy and sorrow. When I pray the Psalms, I remember that I am joining in the same prayers that the people of God have voiced for some 3,000 years. The Psalms teach us to bring our sorrow and frustration to God in lament, to overflow with thanksgiving at answered prayer, and to proclaim God's greatness to a world that desperately needs to hear.

My prayer for you is that this book will help you to grow in your ability to relate to God in joy and sorrow. That you would grow in your sense of wonder at God's faithfulness, grace, and justice.

That you will be inspired to express gratitude to God for what He has done. And that you would long for the return of the Lord Jesus when we will be able to worship together in God's presence.

Dr. Ryan Cook
Author and Professor, Moody Theological Seminary

BOOK 1

PSALMS 1–41

BOOK 1

> PSALM 1

Delight in God's Word

The Lord watches over the way of the righteous, but the way of the wicked leads to destruction.

PSALM 1:6

What comes to mind when you think of "the good life"? Many of us might picture a life filled with family and friends, healthy bodies, and financial security. Or we might look to achievements like leading a profitable business or being recognized for service in the community.

Psalm 1 opens with the word "blessed," which can also be translated as "happy" (v. 1). The psalmist paints a picture of someone living the "good life." What does true happiness look like? It is not what you might think. This psalm does not celebrate financial prosperity or outstanding achievements. Rather, the blessed person is someone who delights in and meditates on God's law (v. 2).

The word "meditate" might make us think of time spent in silent reflection. But the word is most often used in the Bible to refer to low animal sounds—the cooing of a pigeon or the growl of a lion (Isa. 31:4; 38:14). To meditate is to ruminate on or constantly talk about God's Word. Dwelling on God's Word is this person's singular passion.

This person is beautifully described as a tree planted by streams of water (v. 3). This secure position means the tree is fruitful and endures, even in times of drought. A fruitful tree provides shelter and food for many. In a similar way, the person who delights in God's law will be a blessing to others. By contrast, the wicked are like chaff; unfruitful, useless, and transient. Instead of listening to and delighting in God's Word, they mock and scoff at others (v. 1). Their way of life leads to death (v. 5).

"Having it all," according to the Bible, means being joyfully dependent upon God and spending regular time in His Word (v. 2). This good life was modeled for us by the Lord Jesus, who brought healing and refreshment to all who sought Him in faith and whose message was vindicated by His resurrection from the dead.

Go Deeper
What do you look to for happiness? How does reading God's Word contribute to a true sense of blessing or happiness?

Pray with Us
God, as we open the Psalms to learn from Your Word, we ask that You meet us here. Turn our hearts toward You above all else. Help us realize that true joy and happiness is found only in You. Amen.

BOOK 1

PSALM 2

Delight in God's King

> *I will proclaim the* Lord's *decree: He said to me, "You are my son; today I have become your father."*
>
> PSALM 2:7

At the entrance to Solomon's Temple stood two twenty-eight-and-a-half-foot tall bronze pillars. These pillars were elaborately decorated with capitals in the shape of lilies (1 Kings 7:15–22). Each pillar was given a name: Jachin and Boaz. They served as a grand gateway into the temple where the presence of the Lord dwelled.

In a similar way, Psalms 1 and 2 serve as a sort of gateway. These psalms welcome readers into a special temple of praise, the Psalter. They begin and end with a blessing (1:1; 2:12) and share several keywords. They also introduce the two most prominent themes in the Psalter: God's law and God's Messiah.

In Psalm 1, we saw the importance of delighting in God's Word. In Psalm 2, the focus shifts to God's King. The psalm opens with a vivid picture of nations and kings plotting and scheming against God and his anointed King (vv. 1–2). Instead of delighting in God's rule and in His Word, their deepest desire is to break free from them (v. 3). They view them as chains and shackles instead of life-giving, precious gifts. They want to live by their own standards and answer to no one higher than themselves.

While we might be afraid of what human rulers and nations can do, God is not intimidated: "The One enthroned in heaven laughs; the Lord scoffs at them" (v. 4). God declares that He has given over these nations to His Son and Messiah as an inheritance (vv. 6–8). The Lord warns these hostile nations that their best course of action is to "serve the LORD with fear and celebrate his rule with trembling" (v. 11). True wisdom would be to submit to the rule of God and His Messiah while they have the chance . . . or face judgment (v. 12).

The psalm closes with a word of blessing upon those who take refuge in the Lord's Messiah (v. 12). The truly blessed life is found in delighting in God's Word and trusting in His Messiah, the Lord Jesus to whom one day every knee will bow and tongue confess that He is Lord (Phil. 2:10–11).

Go Deeper

What would it look like for you to take refuge in Jesus? Why do you think taking refuge in Him is the way to the blessed life? What other things are you tempted to turn to as a source of safety and security?

Pray with Us

We thank You, Almighty God, that You are our refuge. You are our strength. In You alone do we find true comfort and peace. When times of trouble come, remind us to turn first to You. Amen.

BOOK 1

PSALM 3

The Lies of the Enemy

I call out to the LORD, and he answers me from his holy mountain.

PSALM 3:4

In the garden of Eden, the serpent did not get Adam and Eve to disobey God's command by overpowering them with brute force. Instead, he used one of his most powerful weapons—words: "Did God really say . . . ?" (Gen. 3:1); "You will not certainly die" (Gen. 3:4). These lies sowed doubt about God's goodness and truthfulness and had devastating consequences. The evil one still uses lies today.

In Psalm 3, King David is surrounded by enemies. "LORD, how many are my foes! How many rise up against me!" (v. 1). These enemies had a message to convey: "Many are saying of me, 'God will not deliver him'" (v. 2). David's enemies wanted to convince David that God had abandoned him. It certainly may have looked that way. The preface to the psalm informs us that it was written when David's son Absalom had usurped the throne and driven David out of Jerusalem. How jarring it must have been for David to see most of the nation turn on him and follow his rebellious son. He found himself back on the run in the wilderness as he had been in the days of Saul. How easy it would be to believe the taunts of the crowd that God was not with him.

But David turned his eyes away from his enemies and onto the Lord. "But you, LORD, are a shield around me, my glory, the One who lifts my head high" (v. 3). He was able to sleep in peace because he knew his life was in God's hands (vv. 5–6). In faith, he asked God to defeat his enemies and "break the teeth of the wicked" (v. 7). David ended by affirming that "from the LORD comes deliverance" (v. 8). This psalm teaches that our identity is not found in the acclaim or ridicule of the crowd, but in our relationship with God. David refused to be defined by his enemies and was quick to contradict them.

Go Deeper
Do you find yourself believing the words of people who are trying to harm you? Today, find your identity and hope in the Lord who promises to deliver us.

Pray with Us
Loving God, You know the situations we are facing right now. And we can trust that You are more powerful than any enemy or any situation we may face. Help us trust in You even when the way before us seems dark. We believe in You! Amen.

PSALM 4

Turn Your Eyes upon Yahweh

In peace I will lie down and sleep, for you alone, LORD, make me dwell in safety.

PSALM 4:8

My father-in-law was a farmer. My wife remembers how, at lunchtime, her dad would turn on the radio to hear the current price of grain along with the weather report. While farmers work hard and use a storehouse of wisdom and skill to grow their crops, they also depend on forces outside their control like weather patterns and market prices.

In Psalm 4, David was in a difficult spot. He begged God to "have mercy on me and hear my prayer" (v. 1). The situation seems to be that there was a threat of a bad harvest. In this situation, many in ancient Israel were tempted to worship other gods. The Canaanites believed that Baal, the storm god, was the one to look to for help with crops. Many in Israel were tempted to go along with them.

David laments, "How long will you love delusions and seek false gods?" (v. 2). False gods may promise a lot, but they cannot deliver. David affirms that Yahweh, the God of Israel, will hear when His children cry out to Him (v. 3). Instead of looking to other gods, the people should turn their eyes to the Lord (vv. 4–5). God's presence among His people is even more important than abundant crops (v. 6). Even if the crops of idolators seem to flourish, David proclaims to God, "You have put more joy in my heart than they have when their grain and wine abound" (v. 7 ESV).

When life seems precarious, it can be tempting to take our eyes off the Lord and look for other sources of safety and security. We may not worship Baal like Israel was tempted to do, but we have our own gods. David reminds us that the true source of peace is found in the Lord alone (v. 8). As Jesus reminded us, "But seek first his kingdom and his righteousness, and all these things will be given to you as well" (Matt. 6:33).

Go Deeper

Do you find yourself tempted to take your eyes off the Lord when confronted by the needs around you? How does David try to turn Israel back to God in this psalm? How can that be a model for us?

Pray with Us

Lord Jesus, help us never take our eyes off You. Like Peter walking on water, we tend to be distracted by the waves. But when we turn our eyes to You, Jesus, we find comfort and hope and peace. Keep us focused on You alone. Amen.

BOOK 1

PSALM 5

Waiting on God

In the morning, Lord, you hear my voice; in the morning I lay my requests before you and wait expectantly.

PSALM 5:3

Passengers at a Houston airport were complaining about how long they had to wait at the baggage claim. So, airport executives hired more baggage handlers and cut the wait time to eight minutes. However, the complaints did not stop. Airport executives then tried a different approach. They moved the baggage claim so it was a seven-minute walk from the arrival gates. The complaints stopped.

Waiting for an answer to our prayers can be difficult and painful. In Psalm 5, David cried out to the Lord, laid his requests before Him, and then waited expectantly (v. 3). David's particular problem was his enemies. Men were making false accusations against him (v. 9). These men were arrogant, bloodthirsty, and rebellious against God (vv. 5, 6, 10). It was so difficult that it caused David to lament (v. 1). The word translated *lament* literally means "groan" or "sigh," a kind of confused muttering that comes from the depths of an anguished soul.

Amid suffering, David held on to hope. He knew God and trusted in His character. God was not "pleased with wickedness" (v. 4). He could not stand the arrogant and wrongdoer (v. 5). He detested the bloodthirsty and deceitful (v. 6). He had also made a covenant commitment to David (v. 7). David asked God to be true to His character. That He would denounce the guilty and protect the faithful (vv. 10–11). But it was just that—a request. God would be the one to act in his defense.

We have all experienced times when life feels desperate. In those times, we can do what David modeled in this psalm. We can be honest with God about our plight. We can pray according to God's attributes. And we can wait for God to act. Our hope is grounded in the character of God. There is no surer foundation than that.

Go Deeper

Why is it so difficult for us to wait for answers to our prayers? How does Psalm 5 encourage us in the waiting?

Pray with Us

Dear Lord, we find it so hard to wait! Impatience creeps into so many areas of our lives, from the ordinary delays of waiting in line to the significant waits involving broken relationships or answers to health concerns. Be with us in the waiting, Lord, and remind us to turn to You in prayer. Amen.

BOOK 1

PSALM 6

Not Too Proud to Beg

The LORD has heard my cry for mercy; the LORD accepts my prayer.

PSALM 6:9

Navy SEALs undergo a rigorous physical and mental trial appropriately named "Hell Week." The new recruits are constantly in motion. They run, swim, do sit-ups and push-ups, endure cold water, and accomplish difficult tasks, all on minimal sleep! Some can endure this experience only because they know the end is in sight.

David is at his breaking point in this psalm. He does not see an end in sight. "How long, LORD, how long?" he asks (v. 3). He seems to have been suffering a sickness of some sort. He laments that he is "faint" and that his "bones are in agony" (v. 2). He understands this affliction is the result of God's punishment for his sin. He begged God not to discipline or rebuke him in His anger, not because he is innocent, but out of mercy (v. 2).

David gives two reasons for God to have compassion. He asks, "Among the dead no one proclaims your name. Who praises you from the grave?" (v. 5). He reasons that God should spare his life so he can praise God. This may seem like an odd reason. However, it reveals a deep theological truth. For David, life consisted of praising the Lord. Not to praise God is in a sense not to be fully alive.

David asks God to restore his health so he could return to this important calling.

Second, David paints a vivid picture of his suffering in order to arouse God's compassion. "All night long I flood my bed with weeping and drench my couch with tears" (v. 6). David believes that God cares about his suffering. He ends his lament with a note of faith: "The Lord has heard my cry for mercy; the Lord accepts my prayer" (v. 9).

Go Deeper

Do you relate to David, feeling worn out by your sorrow? How does this psalm help you express your pain and plea to God?

Pray with Us

Lord, like the psalmist, we are worn out. Our bed is flooded with tears. When we are at our breaking point, consumed by worry, turn our hearts and minds to You. Give us Your peace that passes all understanding (Phil. 4:7). You are our refuge and strength (Ps. 46:1). Amen.

BOOK 1

PSALM 7

God of Justice

My shield is God Most High, who saves the upright in heart.

PSALM 7:10

Seventeen-year-old Shareef Cousin found himself the youngest person in the United States on death row. Shareef had been convicted of murder even though he had what seemed like an airtight alibi. Afterward it was determined that the detective on the case lied to obtain an arrest warrant. The only actual eyewitness to the crime had mistakenly identified Shareef as guilty. Shareef served four years in prison before the verdict was overturned, and he was set free.

In this psalm, David laments that a certain Cush had falsely accused him of crimes. We do not know any specifics about this situation from the Bible, but based on this psalm it is clear that David was being accused of betraying a friend and of robbery (v. 4). This puts David in a precarious position. He describes his accuser as a lion who wanted to "rip me to pieces" (v. 2). In this stressful situation, David pleads for God's help.

David appealed to God's justice. He knew that God is perfectly righteous and that no secret was hidden from Him. God can probe the "minds and hearts" of any person (v. 9). David asked God to be true to His character and vindicate him from the injustice and rage of his enemies (v. 6). David put his hope in God as his "shield" and protector (v. 10).

David also expressed his trust in the moral structure of the world God created. He proclaimed, "Whoever is pregnant with evil conceives trouble and gives birth to disillusionment. Whoever digs a hole and scoops it out falls into the pit they have made" (vv. 14–15). David knew that, in general, we reap what we sow. Because of this, he gives thanks to the Lord and says he will "sing the praises of the name of the LORD Most High" (v. 17), even while facing injustice.

Go Deeper

Have you ever been falsely accused? What can we ask of the Lord when we face injustice in our lives? What can we trust He will do?

Pray with Us

Lord of justice, thank You for Your salvation that is extended to everyone who calls on Your name. May we remember, even when facing life's wrongs, that Your justice will ultimately be achieved. Amen.

BOOK 1

> PSALM 8

God of Wonders

Lord, our Lord, how majestic is your name in all the earth!
You have set your glory in the heavens.

PSALM 8:1

In 2009, Susan Boyle achieved international fame for her audition on *Britain's Got Talent*. She did not seem like the usual contestant. She was forty-seven years old and unemployed, and no one expected much from her—until she began to sing. Her brilliant rendition of "I Dreamed a Dream" became the most watched video on YouTube that year, and Susan went on to sell millions of albums.

When we encounter the unexpected, we respond with a sense of wonder. In Psalm 8, David praises God, not for His power or might, but for how He often uses the people we least expect. In verse 2 David proclaims, "Through the praise of children and infants you have established a stronghold against your enemies, to silence the foe and the avenger." In the ancient world with high infant mortality rates, babies were a symbol of powerlessness and fragility. So, David glorifies God because He uses the praise of the most insignificant, weak, and needy people in society to silence His enemies. God is shown to be majestic because of how He chooses the weak to silence the strong.

God has always enjoyed working in this way. In verses 3 and 4, David reflects on how vast the created universe was and how God put all these wonders under the care and authority of humans. How small we seem compared to elephants or supernovas! Yet, "you made them rulers over the works of your hands; you put everything under their feet" (v. 6).

This theme of God showing His strength in weakness comes to its ultimate fulfillment on the cross. When Jesus was at His weakest point, beaten and mocked and hanging on a Roman cross, he was accomplishing the most. In His death, He defeated His enemies: the power of sin and Satan and death.

Go Deeper

Have you ever felt too weak or insignificant to be used by God? Can you think of one person in the Bible who seemed too insignificant to be chosen by God? How did He use them?

Pray with Us

Lord Jesus, we confess that sometimes we consider ourselves too weak and too insignificant to serve You well. We wonder why You would want to use someone like us. Remind us that Your strength is made perfect in our weakness. Help us follow You faithfully. Amen.

BOOK 1

PSALM 9

The ABCs of Praise and Lament: Part 1

I will give thanks to you, LORD, with all my heart; I will tell of all your wonderful deeds.

PSALM 9:1

In the preface to his commentary on the Psalms, John Calvin describes the book in this way: "I have been accustomed to call this book . . . 'An Anatomy of all the Parts of the Soul'; for there is not an emotion of which any one can be conscious that is not here represented as a mirror."[4] The Psalms are a true reflection of the life we experience in a fallen world.

Psalms 9 and 10 belong together as one psalm in two parts. Psalm 9 is the first half of an acrostic that runs through Psalm 10. David begins with a rousing call to give thanks to the Lord (Ps. 9:1–2). He calls on people everywhere to rejoice because the Lord has defeated his enemies, established justice, and been a refuge for the poor and oppressed (vv. 3–10). David has experienced the truth that God does not forsake His children (v. 10). One of the ways that the Lord defeats the wicked is by allowing them to reap the natural results of their own actions, "the wicked are ensnared by the work of their hands" (v. 16). The Lord reigns and "does not ignore the cries of the afflicted" (v. 12). The proper response to God's deliverance is to celebrate his deliverance with God's people in worship (v. 14).

With David, we can give thanks to the Lord that He has defeated our enemies. At the cross, Jesus "disarmed the powers and authorities" (Col. 2:15). However, like David, we still struggle against "the powers of this dark world" (Eph. 6:12). At times we can long for justice and pray with David, "Arise, Lord, do not let mortals triumph; let the nations be judged in your presence" (v. 19). We can place our hope in the victory that has already been achieved. One day we will be able to sing, "The kingdom of the world has become the kingdom of our Lord and of his Messiah, and he will reign for ever and ever" (Rev. 11:15).

Go Deeper

Right now, even as we await Jesus' second coming and for all wrongs to be made right, are there times you have seen God provide a measure of justice in your life? What are ways in which God has met your needs that you can tell someone about today?

Pray with Us

It is so easy to get impatient, Lord. We wonder when You will return and when Your justice will prevail. Give us patience as we wait. Help us trust that You will return at the right time to right all wrongs. Amen.

PSALM 10

The ABCs of Praise and Lament: Part 2

But you, God, see the trouble of the afflicted; you consider their grief and take it in hand. The victims commit themselves to you; you are the helper of the fatherless.

PSALM 10:14

The Bible is honest and straightforward about the evil and human suffering that exists in this fallen world. God does not ask us to pretend like the world is better than it is. But Scripture does help us understand what God has done and how He will bring about judgment and redemption. Until that day, He has given us models of how to relate to Him in faith.

Psalm 10 is the second half of an acrostic poem that began in Psalm 9. In yesterday's reading, David gave thanks to God for his salvation. In this portion of the psalm, his thanksgiving shifts to lament. Even though God had rescued David in the past, there was a new enemy who needed to be confronted. This man hunted down the vulnerable, was arrogant, and had "no room for God" in his thoughts (v. 4). He rejected God's law and prospered by abusing the "innocent" and "helpless" (vv. 5, 8–10). This man justified his behavior by saying to himself, "God will never notice; he covers his face and never sees" (v. 11). He lived as if there was no God. David begged God to "arise" and "not forget the helpless" (v. 12). David knew that God cares for the vulnerable, poor, and helpless from many places in Scripture (Deut. 15:10–11). He wondered, "Why, Lord, do you stand far off? Why do you hide yourself in times of trouble?" (v. 1).

By at the end of the psalm, David affirmed his confidence in God. The Lord hears "the desire of the afflicted" and listens "to their cry" (v. 17). David had seen God answer prayer in the past and he trusts Him for the future. The wicked would not get away with it forever. One day, all people will give an account before the Judge of all the earth. In this one poem, David travels from thanksgiving to lament and back again to rest in a place of hope.

Go Deeper

Have you ever been deeply troubled by the sheer amount of suffering and evil in the world? This psalm encourages us to take those thoughts to God and pray for Him to intervene. He sees, cares, and will one day make all things new.

Pray with Us

Lord, like David, we struggle with the afflictions of this world. And like David, we place our hope in You. Thank You that echoing Psalm 10, we can say the Lord hears "the desires of the afflicted." Amen.

BOOK 1

> PSALM 11

Flight or Faith

For the LORD *is righteous, he loves justice; the upright will see his face.*

PSALM 11:7

Thomas Edison was determined to invent a commercially viable electric light bulb. He knew the value it would bring to the average person. Yet after countless failed attempts, his friends and family began to ask if he was ready to give up. The story is told of a newspaper reporter who asked Edison if he felt like a failure. Edison replied, "I have not failed. I've just found 10,000 ways that won't work."[5]

In today's psalm, David faced adversity. We do not know exactly what trial he was facing, but it was significant enough that people around him encouraged him to "flee like a bird to your mountain" (v. 1). Their advice was to run away! After all, wicked men were dangerous. They hid in the shadows and attempted to assassinate the righteous (v. 2). David's problems were not just these men, but that the very foundations of society were being destroyed (v. 3). The moral order had fallen away. What could a righteous person do but run?

David had an answer. Instead of running, we can choose to look up. "The LORD is in his holy temple; the LORD is on his heavenly throne" (v. 4). The wicked may seem like they are getting away with murder. It may look like there is no hope for the upright. But

David knew that was not the full picture. The Lord sits on the throne and will hold the wicked accountable. He is not aloof to human oppression, but carefully examines "everyone on earth" (v. 4). In His justice, He will judge the wicked and uphold the upright. We can trust in this because the Lord "hates" evil, but "loves justice" (vv. 5, 7). We can choose faith in our incorruptible God.

Go Deeper

As we look at the society around us, it may seem like our very foundation is being destroyed. Christian values are not only ignored, but in many sectors of society viewed as a problem. How does this psalm direct us to respond?

Pray with Us

Lord Jesus, we pray we'll listen to the teaching in today's Scripture reading. As Psalm 11 encourages us, we pray we'll choose faith in You and find our consolation and refuge in Your love. Amen.

PSALM 12

Surrounded by Lies

The words of the LORD are flawless, like silver purified in a crucible, like gold refined seven times.

PSALM 12:6

In 2002, a researcher from the University of Massachusetts studied how often people lie during daily conversations. He found that 60 percent of adults could not get through a ten-minute conversation without lying at least once.[6] Most people lied three times. It can feel like we are surrounded by lies.

In Psalm 12, David lamented that "everyone lies to their neighbor" (v. 2). He knew that outright lies were not the only problem. He also described flattery, boasting, and manipulation (vv. 2–3). The reason people are deceptive with their speech is because it can help achieve desired results. When Satan wanted to entice Eve to eat of the forbidden fruit in the garden, he did it through deceptive speech. David's adversaries in this psalm boast, "By our tongues we will prevail; our own lips will defend us—who is lord over us?" (v. 4).

When powerful people practice deception, it is often the poor and vulnerable who suffer. In this psalm, God answers David's lament. "Because the poor are plundered and the needy groan, I will now arise" (v. 5). The deceptive speech of the enemy is countered by God's Word. Not only did God answer David's prayer in this particular situation, but we also know that in the end justice will be achieved for all. Liars will not win in the end. Our hope is in the promise of Christ's return to judge the living and the dead. We can rest in this certain hope because it is promised in God's Word. His Word is not like the empty words of deceivers, but "like silver purified in a crucible, like gold refined seven times" (v. 6). In Psalm 119, the psalmist declares, "I delight in your commands because I love them" (v. 47). God's Word is a precious gift.

Go Deeper

In a world full of lies, why is the reading and understanding of Scripture so important? Take a few minutes today to thank the Lord for His perfect and life-giving Word.

Pray with Us

How true Your Word is, God. You see the lying that surrounds us. It is sometimes difficult to know who we can believe. We ask that You cut through the confusion and guide us with Your Holy Spirit. Teach us the right way, God. Help us stay on the right path. Amen.

BOOK 1

PSALM 13

Lament as Grief

But I trust in your unfailing love; my heart rejoices in your salvation.

PSALM 13:5

In 2014, psychologists from the University of Virginia in Charlottesville conducted an experiment. They put students in a room and told them that, if they wanted to, they could push a button and shock themselves. The results were surprising. Sixty-seven percent of the men and 25 percent of the women chose to shock themselves rather than sit quietly and think.[7]

Many people feel it is hard to be alone and even harder to be abandoned. David began this lament asking four times, "How long?" David wanted reassurance that God still cared. He wanted God to act in his defense. He was surrounded by enemies who wanted to gloat over his demise, and David felt abandoned by God.

When we feel abandoned, we might think that God does not want to help us. We may begin to doubt the existence of God altogether. David did not go down either of these roads. Instead, he waited. It was a waiting filled with questions and pleas. Waiting does not necessarily mean sitting quietly. It is one way of being faithful to God even in the midst of sorrow (v. 2).

But David also waited in hope. He trusted in God's covenant commitment to him and anticipated God's salvation (v. 5). He remembered what God had done for him in the past (v. 6). It is possible to be full of grief and hope at the same time. The apostle Paul reminded the church at Thessalonica, "We do not want you to be uninformed... so that you do not grieve like the rest of mankind, who have no hope" (1 Thess. 4:13). David here reminds us that God is worth clinging to even when we do not sense His presence. Remember that even our Lord cried the words of a lament psalm, "My God, My God why have you forsaken me?" (Matt. 27:46).

Go Deeper

Are you are walking through a time of anxiety or trouble? How does this psalm speak into your situation?

Pray with Us

Today, Lord God, we bring our troubles before You. You know the situation we are facing from the inside out. We trust You for the solution. Help us not to trust our feelings, especially when we feel abandoned. Instead, Lord, we trust in You and Your Word. Amen.

BOOK 1

> PSALM 14

Practical Atheism

The fool says in his heart, "There is no God." They are corrupt, their deeds are vile; there is no one who does good.

PSALM 14:1

"Practical atheism" is a term that refers to someone who lives as if there is no God regardless of what they may say. They may give lip service to God's existence, but when it comes down to it, they live as if there is no God to worship, honor, and obey.

The person described in the opening of Psalm 14 is a practical atheist. Whatever they may say they believe, in their heart of hearts their life is oriented by the conviction, "There is no God" (v. 1). David calls this person a fool. The fool's beliefs have consequences. Practical atheism leads to vile deeds, corruption, and an inability to do good (v. 1). This attitude is pervasive; "The LORD looks down from heaven on all mankind to see if there are any who understand, any who seek God" (v. 2). The conclusion is bleak—"All have turned away" (v. 3).

The primary difference between the righteous and the wicked in the book of Psalms is that the righteous live in fear of God. This does not mean they cringe in terror before God, but that they recognize that there is a God who will hold them accountable. He is a God before whom "no secrets are hid."[8] The wicked by contrast live as if there is no God and no accountability. Not surprisingly this leads to suffering, especially for the poor (v. 6).

But there is another reality at work in the world as well. Despite the hopes of the fool, there is a God who sees and who will judge. The Lord is a refuge for His people (v. 6). The folly and evil of the world should make us long with David for God's salvation to shine forth (v. 7). While it is true that "all have sinned and fall short of the glory of God" (Rom. 3:23), in Christ, "the gift of God is eternal life" (Rom. 6:23). We can be grateful that "while we were still sinners, Christ died for us" (Rom. 5:8).

Go Deeper

Can you resonate at all with the practical atheist? How different would your life look if you did not believe in God? How might this psalm be a source of hope?

Pray with Us

God, we come before You ashamed of the times we live as if You do not exist. We may not say those words, but we can go about our days without reflecting on Your purpose and Your will. Guide us. Keep us. Forgive us. Amen.

BOOK 1

PSALM 15

Invitation to Worship

He has shown you, O mortal, what is good. And what does the LORD *require of you? To act justly and to love mercy and to walk humbly with your God.*

MICAH 6:8

In July 2017, Canada's governor general found himself embroiled in controversy. While descending steps alongside the Queen of England, he touched the Queen's elbow to assist her. What was meant as an act of service was actually a breach of protocol.[9] When meeting the Queen, there are clear guidelines regarding what kind of behavior and actions are appropriate.

In the Old Testament, worshiping the Lord involved certain rituals. Psalm 15 was likely intended as a question-and-answer psalm for those coming to the sanctuary. When David asks, "LORD, who may dwell in your sacred tent?" (v. 1), the Lord replies with a list of eleven characteristics that focus not on external practices, but internal behavior.

The first characteristic is the most general: "One whose walk is blameless, who does what is righteous" (v. 2). This does not mean a worshiper must be sinless. Indeed, most people who came to the sanctuary were offering a sacrifice for their sin. Instead, to be blameless meant to have a heart of repentance, one that feared

God. The blameless life manifests itself in purity of speech. This person does not "slander" others, but "speaks the truth from their heart" (vv. 2–3).

The blameless person honors the people who fear God while rejecting those who despise Him (v. 4). The blameless are true to their word, even when it is to their disadvantage (v. 4). The blameless care for the poor. They lend money to the poor without interest. God cares deeply about how we treat the poor and vulnerable. He affirms that this is the kind of person who is welcome to worship in His presence. While it is true that we can come "just as we are" to salvation, the worship of God in His presence should not be taken lightly or casually (Matt. 5:23–24; 1 Cor. 11:27–32).

Go Deeper

What matters most to God in our worship? How do we balance coming to God "just as I am" with being mindful of His holiness?

Pray with Us

Our Father, we come before You, overwhelmed by Your holiness. In Your presence, we are aware of how often we fall short. Help us, by the power of Your Spirit, to be "blameless," to walk in a manner worthy of our calling. Amen.

BOOK 1

PSALM 16

Count Your Blessings

You make known to me the path of life; you will fill me with joy in your presence, with eternal pleasures at your right hand.

PSALM 16:11

When I was a child, we used to sing the hymn "Count Your Blessings." The first verse was, "When upon life's billows you are tempest tossed; When you are discouraged thinking all is lost; Count your many blessings, name them one by one; And it will surprise you what the Lord has done." This is very practical advice. When we face discouragement, we need to step back and remember all the ways the Lord has been faithful.

In Psalm 16, David enumerates four gifts of God for which he is grateful. The first is God Himself. He confesses to the Lord, "You are my Lord; apart from you I have no good thing" (v. 2). The fact that God has made a way to be in relationship with His people is a precious gift. In God alone is true joy to be found (v. 11). The second gift David reminds himself of is the gift of being in community with God's people. He delights in worshiping with fellow believers (v. 3). We were not meant to live the life of faith alone.

The third gift is that of God's Word. He proclaims, "I will praise the Lord, who counsels me; even at night my heart instructs me" (v. 7). This recalls the blessed man of Psalm 1, who meditates upon the law of the Lord "day and night" (Ps. 1:2). Instead of looking at and being overwhelmed by his circumstances, David resolves, "I keep my eyes always on the LORD" (Ps. 16:8).

The fourth gift is David's hope that God's faithfulness will extend beyond the grave. He tells the Lord, "You will not abandon me to the realm of the dead, nor will you let your faithful one see decay" (v. 10). David knows the grave is not the end. His hope is fulfilled in Christ, who defeated death through resurrection. As the apostle Paul put it, "For as in Adam all die, so in Christ all will be made alive" (1 Cor. 15:22). David's hope was not in vain.

Go Deeper

What would your list of things you are grateful for look like? Read through your list. How does naming these blessings help change your perspective?

Pray with Us

May we never forget the many ways You have blessed us, God. Like the psalmist, we thank You most of all for our relationship with You: "Apart from you I have no good thing" (v. 2). Help us never to forget the ways You have blessed us! Amen.

BOOK 1

> PSALM 17

Your Kingdom Come

As for me, I will be vindicated and will see your face; when I awake, I will be satisfied with seeing your likeness.

PSALM 17:15

Children have an innate sense of fairness. If you give a piece of cake to each of two siblings, they will make sure they did not get the smaller one. If one child gets a consequence for misbehavior, they will make sure their brother or sister gets the same treatment.

In Psalm 17, David was surrounded by adversaries. While the cause is not entirely clear, it seems these enemies were falsely accusing him of wrongdoing. They were looking for every opportunity to take David down (vv. 10–12). The primary problem with the wicked is that they believe that their "reward is in this life" (v. 14). They do not think that God will hold them accountable, or that there is judgment after death. In contrast, David declared that he had lived a holy life. "Though you probe my heart . . . you will find that I have planned no evil" (v. 3). He was not saying he was perfect, but rather that he feared God. When he sinned, he repented and called out to God for help. He lived as a man who knew he would one day give account to God. That is the essence of what it means to fear God. David begged God to rescue him from the wicked and to vindicate him from false charges (v. 15).

Even more than getting justice, David wanted to experience God's presence. This desire is clear from his opening plea (v. 1). In the middle of the psalm, he asked God to "keep me as the apple of your eye; hide me in the shadow of your wings" (v. 8). He ended by declaring, "When I awake, I will be satisfied with seeing your likeness" (v. 15). You could summarize David's prayer this way: "May the wicked be far from me, and may You be close."

Go Deeper
Does evil seem to be circling around you? How can you, like David, ask God for His protection and His justice?

Pray with Us
Life can seem so unfair sometimes, Lord. We confess that it is easy to get consumed with our own interests. We worry about our status, our possessions, our safety. Psalm 17 reminds us that You hide us under the shadow of Your wings. Nothing escapes Your notice. Amen.

BOOK 1

> PSALM 18

Rescued at Last

For who is God besides the LORD*? And who is the Rock except our God?*
PSALM 18:31

In 2010 a mine in Chile collapsed, trapping thirty-three miners over 2,000 feet underground. An international rescue team worked around the clock, drilling exploratory holes to locate the missing men. After seventeen days, when food and water were running short, the miners were discovered. Imagine the relief and joy they felt when they realized that rescue was at hand!

For many years, David had run from King Saul. After Saul's death, it took seven years before David's reign was established over the whole nation. We can imagine the relief he felt when he was finally at peace. In Psalm 18, David expressed thanks to God. He declared his love for the Lord, who had proven himself faithful as "my rock, my fortress and my deliverer . . . my shield and the horn of my salvation, my stronghold" (v. 2).

David painted a vivid picture of the kinds of trouble he faced, "the cords of death entangled me, the torrents of destruction overwhelmed me" (v. 4). This terrifying image is answered by an equally vivid picture of the Lord answering his plea for help: "He parted the heavens and came down; dark clouds were under his feet. He mounted the cherubim and flew; he soared on the wings of the wind" (vv. 9–10). No foe was able to stand against the Lord who rescued His anointed.

David's experience led him to praise God's Word and to recognize how unique the Lord is. "For who is God besides the LORD? And who is the Rock except our God?" (v. 31). David recognized that the Lord is our only real hope for security. Sometimes our troubles can seem so overwhelming that we cannot see a way out. David portrays his situation as being at death's door. Yet, he knew that God was his salvation. God would provide a way of escape.

Go Deeper

How does this psalm apply to a difficult situation you are facing? What does it encourage you to do?

Pray with Us

Dear God, we can easily relate to David who faced overwhelming problems. He describes his situation saying that the "cords of death" entangled him. Sometimes life's problems seem too much for us, God. We need You to untangle the mess. Rescue us! Help us, God! Amen.

BOOK 1

PSALM 19

Speaking of His Wonder

The heavens declare the glory of God; the skies proclaim the work of his hands.

PSALM 19:1

According to the National Solar Observatory, the core temperature of the sun is 27 million degrees Fahrenheit. Every second of every day, the sun releases five million tons of pure energy.[10] Consider that the sun is one of trillions of stars in the sky, which were created when God spoke, "Let there be lights in the vault of the sky" (Gen. 1:14).

Psalm 19 celebrates the truth that it is possible for us to know the Creator of the heavens and the earth. One way we can learn truth about God is by opening our eyes and looking at the world around us. Just like a painting can reveal truth about the artist, the stars and mountains, woods and streams reveal truth about the One who spoke them into being. David declares, "Day after day they pour forth speech" (v. 2). The phrase "pour forth" is used of a spring bubbling up out of the ground. It is as if the heavens are bubbling over, jabbering away about God.

In the second half of the psalm, David declares that we can know God through His Word. It is perfect and refreshing to the soul (v. 7). If we had to choose between Scripture and a heap of gold, the obvious choice is God's Word. In addition to giving us wisdom, joy, and life, it warns us of danger and keeps us from errors (v. 11).

Most people in life desire money and pleasure. David here proclaims that Scripture meets both needs. The Word of God is sweeter than honey and more precious than gold. David concludes by thinking about his own speech. He recognizes how pure and true the words of Scripture are and prays that his own words will mirror those same qualities (v. 14).

Go Deeper

When was the last time you watched a sunset or viewed the stars at night? Today, take special notice of the beauty of this created world and praise God!

Pray with Us

Today, our Father, we give You praise. We thank You for the beauty that surrounds us, for the sun that gives us light by day and the stars that light the night sky. Everywhere we look there is evidence of Your power and Your creativity. We praise You, our magnificent Creator. Amen.

BOOK 1

PSALM 20

God Hears My Cry

Some trust in chariots and some in horses, but we trust in the name of the Lord our God.

PSALM 20:7

As Jesus was on His way to Jerusalem, He encountered ten lepers who begged Him for healing. Jesus answered their request, and in accordance with Mosaic law, instructed the men to show themselves to the priest who would declare them clean. Even so, only one man returned to give praise to God and thank Jesus for His healing touch (Luke 17:11–17).

Psalm 20 reminds us to give thanks to the Lord. Today's passage opens with David on the eve of battle. His people surrounded him, offering a plea on his behalf. They asked that God would "answer you when you are in distress; may the name of the God of Jacob protect you" (v. 1). They asked God to remember the sacrifices and offerings the king had made (v. 3). Ultimately, they prayed for victory.

In the ancient world, it would be tempting for people to put their hope in war horses, chariots or, even better, a mighty army. But Israel knew better. They declared, "Some trust in chariots and some in horses, but we trust in the name of the Lord our God" (v. 7). They remembered the period of the Judges when God raised up deliverers who used weapons like ox goads, donkey jawbones, tent pegs, and clay pots and torches. Salvation did not depend upon military prowess, but upon the Lord's power. David was not slow in giving thanks to the Lord.

Once our prayers are answered, it can be easy to forget to thank God. Other issues press for our time and attention. Even worse, we turn to new needs that arise and fail to reflect on the great things God has done. This psalm reminds us to remember what God has done in our past, and to turn to Him with our needs for the present.

Go Deeper

How has God answered your prayers in the past? Why does reflecting on those answers give you confidence and hope in the future?

Pray with Us

In You alone, God, we place our trust. Nothing else is as dependable or certain. Nothing else can give us hope for the future. Remind us that all answers are found in You alone. Like the psalmist, we "trust in the name of the LORD our God" (v. 7). Amen.

BOOK 1

> PSALM 21

A Victory Song

Be exalted in your strength, LORD; we will sing and praise your might.
PSALM 21:13

Peace is illusive. At the time I am writing this, there are five major wars being fought ("major war" being defined as over ten thousand combat deaths in the past year) in addition to over one hundred other armed conflicts. Despite the efforts of many organizations and diplomats who are sincerely working for peace, war continues to exist and comes at great cost.

Ancient Israel regularly found itself at war. In fact, war was so common that Israel remarked on periods of peace as a joyful respite from the norm (e.g., Judg. 3:11; 2 Chron. 14:1). Psalm 21 is a song of thanksgiving for answered prayer. David had prayed for a military victory, and it was granted. This brought David great joy because it meant that God had been faithful to His promises and that the people of God could continue to worship Him (vv. 1, 6). The victory affirmed God's care and provision for His people.

David knew his victory was not the result of careful military cunning or the strength of his army. Instead, he gave all credit to the Lord (vv. 8–12). David focused his hope in the right place: "For the king trusts in the LORD; through the unfailing love of the Most High he will not be shaken" (v. 7).

While the church is not a political entity or called upon to fight with military arms, we do face dangerous foes. Paul reminds us, "For our struggle is not against flesh and blood, but against the rulers, against the authorities, against the powers of this dark world and against the spiritual forces of evil in the heavenly realms" (Eph. 6:12). Our provisions in this struggle are truth, righteousness, the gospel, faith, salvation, the Spirit, and the Word of God (Eph. 6:13–17). We are called to hope and trust in the victory that the Lord Jesus has achieved for us (Col. 2:13–15). Because of this, we too can voice hymns of praise for what the Lord has done, "Salvation belongs to our God, who sits on the throne, and to the Lamb" (Rev. 7:10).

Go Deeper

Why does war and conflict continue to exist? What does the psalmist express that comforts us in times of personal and societal conflict?

Pray with Us

Conflict is all around us, God. We read it in the headlines. We see battles on social media. We hear it in conversations with friends and families. Like the psalmist we turn to You. We trust "in the LORD; through the unfailing love of the Most High [we] will not be shaken" (v. 7). Amen.

BOOK 1

PSALM 22

From Despair to Hope

All the ends of the earth will remember and turn to the LORD, *and all the families of the nations will bow down before him.*

PSALM 22:27

In the gospel of Mark, Jesus makes only one statement from the cross, "'*Eloi, Eloi, lema sabachthani?*' (which means 'My God, my God, why have you forsaken me?')" (Mark 15:34). Many people understand Jesus' words as a cry of despair. However, for those with ears to hear, this statement is filled with hope. Jesus was not just praying extemporaneously—He was quoting from the opening line of today's reading, Psalm 22.

In verses 1–11, David asks God why He seems so far off. He reminds God that in the past, He delivered the people of Israel (v. 4). Couldn't God show that same salvation now? David was insulted by his enemies (vv. 6–8). He envisioned himself as being surrounded by dangerous animals who were closing in, wanting to tear him apart (vv. 12–13). He was distraught, helpless, to the point of death (v. 15). He begged God to act. "But you, LORD, do not be far from me. You are my strength; come quickly to help me" (v. 19).

However, the psalm takes a sharp turn in verse 22. David's prayer has been heard and salvation has come! He resolves to praise the Lord in the sacred assembly (v. 22). He addresses "all the ends of the earth" and "all the families of the nations" (v. 27). David declares the Lord is the ruler of all the nations. Because of this, all the nations owe their allegiance to Him. This message of salvation is so significant that it even needs to be declared to those who are not born yet (v. 31). When Jesus prayed this psalm on the cross, He was not only giving voice to the grief and pain He felt but also proclaiming the truth that this psalm ends with: Jesus is Lord of all.

Go Deeper

When God answers your prayers, do you praise Him? Consider how you can tell people in your life what He has done for you!

Pray with Us

Dear Jesus, we ask for courage to stand up for what is right. Help us to bravely speak about You in the public spaces. Give us the ability to clearly and confidently communicate Your truth to the people in our lives who need to hear about Your salvation. Amen.

BOOK 1

> PSALM 23

The Good Shepherd

"I am the good shepherd. The good shepherd lays down his life for the sheep."

JOHN 10:11

According to *Time* magazine, the most popular song in the world is the Disney anthem, "It's a Small World."[11] It was written by the Sherman Brothers whom Walt Disney told, "I need one song that can be easily translated into many languages and be played as a round."[12] If you were asked to name the most popular psalm in the world, you would probably answer: Psalm 23. Even in our post-Christian society, most people can quote from the King James Version, "The LORD is my shepherd, I shall not want."

Psalm 23 portrays God in two roles, as shepherd and host. As shepherd, the Lord provides for the needs of His people. David declares, "I lack nothing" (v. 1). It does not mean he gets whatever he wants; it means the Lord will provide everything he needs. In a barren climate, the Lord leads His sheep to "green pastures" and "quiet waters" (v. 1). This consistent care and provision led David to have a deep trust in the Lord. Even when the Lord led him through the "darkest valley," he was not afraid (v. 4). As one commentator put it, "The dark valley . . . is as truly one of his 'right paths' as are the green pastures—a fact that takes much of the sting out of any ordeal."[13] The Lord guides with His shepherd's tools: a staff and a rod.

In verse 5, God is pictured as a gracious host. The Lord invites David to enjoy His hospitality even in the presence of his enemies (v. 5). As a good host, the Lord makes sure that His guest has an anointed head and a full cup (v. 5). David responds with gratitude, confessing that the Lord's "goodness and love" will pursue him throughout his life, and he was confident that he would live with God in His presence forever (v. 6).

Go Deeper

Have you ever wondered if God really sees what you are going through? Does He notice? Does He care? What does today's psalm teach us about God's care for us?

Pray with Us

Because of you, O God, "I lack nothing" (v. 1). When my mind and heart crave more, when I struggle with discontent, remind me of this truth. I can trust in You as my Good Shepherd. You are all I will ever need. Amen.

BOOK 1

PSALM 24

The Owner of All

The earth is the LORD's, and everything in it, the world,
and all who live in it.

PSALM 24:1

As I backed down a driveway one night, I was startled by a loud crash. I had accidently gone off the driveway and backed the car into a large potted plant, leaving a scratch on the rear bumper. If the car had been my own, it would not have been a big deal. However, this particular car was a rental. I would have to give an account of my mistake to someone else.

In today's reading, David reminds us that the world we inhabit and everything in it belong to God. We may sometimes act as if our house, car, possessions, or even our bodies belong to us. The reality is that God created everything and everyone. All creation belongs to Him (vv. 1–2). Israel was reminded of this truth every fiftieth year when all debts were canceled and all property reverted back to its original tribal allotment (Lev. 25). They were not the ultimate owners of the land.

In verses 3–4, David reminds Israel that approaching God in worship is not to be done lightly. He outlines two characteristics of an authorized worshiper. We must have "clean hands and a pure heart" (v. 4). That is, we are to be people who have purity in our motives and in our actions. We must also be loyal to the Lord alone. Our trust cannot be in any of the false gods who so easily attract our attention (v. 4). These are the people who can worship the Lord *and* receive His blessing (v. 5).

The final portion of the psalm calls for the gates of Jerusalem to be prepared to receive the King of glory. Since the whole earth belongs to the Lord, it is appropriate that the psalm ends by anticipating the future coming of the Messiah-King to take up His throne (Matt. 25:31).

Go Deeper

Who is the owner of all? How does this change our perspective on acquiring and keeping our possessions?

Pray with Us

Like a child, I tend to shout, "This is mine!" But the truth is, God, that everything belongs to You. Remind me that I possess nothing. All that I have and all that I am is Yours. Keep me mindful of this truth that brings comfort and peace. Amen.

BOOK 1

PSALM 25

In God We Trust

*Who, then, are those who fear the L*ORD*? He will instruct them in the ways they should choose.*

PSALM 25:12

The Global Positioning System (GPS) is an indispensable part of modern life. This technology was originally developed by the US Department of Defense to assist the military. But today GPS satellites impact most people's daily lives. How else would we find our way?

In Psalm 25, David describes a world that is difficult to navigate. At every turn, he was threatened by enemies (v. 2), snares that could entrap him (v. 15), general afflictions and anxieties (v. 17), and his own sins and iniquity (vv. 7, 11, 18). In this dangerous and confusing world, David looked to God for guidance. "Show me your ways, LORD, teach me your paths" (v. 4). He knew that God "guides the humble in what is right and teaches them his way" (v. 9). God's ways are "loving and faithful" (v. 10). Therefore, David trusted God to lead him in the right direction (v. 12).

David prayed for forgiveness (vv. 11, 18). He knew the dangers he faced were not just the threats of the enemy, but the deceitfulness of his own heart (vv. 7, 11). This knowledge did not lead him to despair, but drove him to God. He was reminded not only of his need for forgiveness but also of his need for a Savior (vv. 5, 15).

David's confession was rooted in his faith in the Lord. "In you, LORD my God, I put my trust" (v. 1). Even while surrounded by dangers and enemies, his "eyes are ever on the LORD" (v. 15). The good news is that this truth is not just for David, but for all of God's people. It can be easy for us to feel overwhelmed by troubles in life. David reminds us to keep our eyes focused on the Lord, who is our only real source of hope.

Go Deeper

David wrote this psalm as an acrostic following the Hebrew alphabet. It is as if David is saying, "Trust God in every circumstance, from A to Z." Can you praise God naming His characteristics from A to Z?

Pray with Us

When I am going to a new location, God, I automatically turn on GPS. How else would I be certain where I was and where I am going? But in life, God, there is no GPS. You alone see the future. You alone know where I should go. Direct and lead me, Lord. Help me to be mindful to always seek You first. Amen.

BOOK 1

> PSALM 26

What Do You Love?

LORD, I love the house where you live, the place where your glory dwells.
PSALM 26:8

Martin Luther once wrote, "Whatever your heart clings to and confides in, that is really your God."[14] What we most love or desire is a good indication of our spiritual health. We naturally pursue that which we most love.

In this psalm, David provides a wonderful model of someone who has his priorities in the right place. He asks God to closely examine his heart (v. 2). He has "always been mindful of your unfailing love and have lived in reliance on your faithfulness" (v. 3). He has lived his life as if God's loving faithfulness was the most important reality.

Because of this, David loves spending time in the temple where God's presence was most clearly manifested in Israel (v. 8). When you love someone, you want to spend as much time with them as you can and look for ways to be with them. David also hates what God hates. He has kept away from "the assembly of evildoers" and refused "to sit with the wicked" (v. 5). He has followed the way of the blessed person (Ps. 1:1).

The reason David is so clearly opening his heart to the Lord is because he is being falsely accused (v. 1). In this way, David's prayer serves as a model for all those who have been unjustly accused of wrongdoing. David is not proclaiming that he is perfect. Instead, he is affirming that his priorities and motives have been shaped by his love for God.

There has only ever been one completely innocent person who suffered unjustly: the Lord Jesus. He did not suffer for His own sin, but for ours. Since we are covered in His righteousness, we can take refuge in Him and pray for God's vindication (Gal. 2:19–21). Through the Spirit, our hearts and minds are being conformed into the image of the Lord Jesus (Rom. 8:29).

Go Deeper

Reflect on the past week. What have you most wanted or pursued? How does Psalm 26 challenge you to adjust your priorities?

Pray with Us

Like the psalmist, we cry, "Test me, LORD, and try me, examine my heart and mind" (v. 2). We praise You, Lord. We dedicate this day to You. Help us to focus on what truly matters. Create in us a longing for Your presence. Amen.

BOOK 1

PSALM 27

The One Thing

> *One thing I ask from the LORD, this only do I seek: that I may dwell in the house of the LORD all the days of my life, to gaze on the beauty of the LORD and to seek him in his temple.*
>
> PSALM 27:4

One of the main reasons for pedestrian fatalities is distracted driving. Most people believe they are pretty good at multitasking. We think we can text, talk on the phone, and drive at the same time. This delusion has made it much more dangerous to cross the street. Sometimes we need to focus on what is most important.

Throughout the Psalms, David is honest in his description of the trials and difficulties of life. In Psalm 27, he talks about enemies, hostile armies, war, oppression, and false accusers. When trials come, it can be easy to be distracted by them. We naturally hustle to put out this fire or that fire. We notice threats coming at us from different quarters and try to meet them. Yet, David reminds us that only one thing is really necessary.

David declares that his one passion is not to defeat his enemy or silence the false accuser, as great as those things would be. Instead, he says, "One thing I ask from the LORD, and this only do I seek: that I may dwell in the house of the LORD all the days of my life" (v. 4). Most of all, he desires intimacy with the Father. He longs to be in God's presence where there is safety, protection, and joy (vv. 5–6).

Time in the presence of God allows David to meet his trials with the proper perspective. He knows there is no person or situation that he needs to fear because God is with him (v. 1). Confident that God will hear his cries for help, David is able to "be strong and take heart and wait for the LORD" (v. 14). We can become so focused on our difficulties that we take our eyes off Jesus. But David reminds us in Psalm 27 to keep our eyes on Him.

Go Deeper

Do you have trouble keeping your eyes on God? Read the story of Peter and Jesus in Matthew 14:29–30. What lesson do we learn here about facing trouble?

Pray with Us

That is me, Lord! I too often let my eyes stray from You. I get distracted by so many things around me. There is so much competing for my attention. Help me to refocus, Lord. Help me to keep my life focused on You alone. Amen.

BOOK 1

PSALM 28

Hear My Cry

The LORD is the strength of his people, a fortress of salvation for his anointed one.

PSALM 28:8

Silence can be a powerful weapon. During conflict, we might use silence as a way of defense or retreat. This is true not only in human relationships but also in our relationship with God. The Psalms model for us ways to engage with God even in the midst of intense suffering.

As David faced a significant trial, he begged God to listen and act. "To you, LORD, I call; you are my Rock, do not turn a deaf ear to me" (v. 1). David had not been silent with God and he asked God to not be silent with him. He is persistent in his prayer, lifting up his hands toward the Most Holy Place (v. 2). We can be thankful that we have a God who does care and who listens to our prayers and responds, even if it does not feel like it in the moment.

David saw people speak peacefully with their neighbors, but "harbor malice in their hearts" (v. 3). Their friendly disposition hid their malicious intent. These people were busy doing evil and did not care about the Lord (vv. 4–5). David asked God to "bring back on them what they deserve" (v. 4). He longed for God's justice.

The tone of the psalm changes abruptly in verse 6. David resounds with praise to the Lord for answered prayer. It seems some time has gone by and David is able to rejoice in what God has done. The depth of his despair is matched by the exuberance of his joy. He closes by asking God to save, bless, and guide Israel (v. 9). David models a way for us to engage with God during difficult times: "Do not turn a deaf ear to me . . . hear my cry for mercy" (vv. 1–2).

Go Deeper

When we experience hardships, it may seem like God is not listening. We may be tempted to go silent. If it feels like God is not listening, why keep praying?

Pray with Us

Even when it feels like You aren't listening, God, we know that You are. Your Word tells us that You hear and that You care. Keep us faithful in times of waiting. Keep us focused on Your truth and Your promises. We trust You with our most troubling situations. Amen.

BOOK 1

PSALM 29

The Lord Is King

The LORD sits enthroned over the flood; the LORD is enthroned as King forever.

PSALM 29:10

According to *National Geographic*, about a hundred lightning bolts strike the earth's surface every second.[15] Despite its commonality, the facts about lightning still boggle the mind. Each bolt of lightning can contain up to one billion volts of electricity. These bolts of energy streak toward the earth at around 200,000 mph, heating the air to five times hotter than the surface of the sun. Lightning is certainly an illuminating example of the power of God.

In the ancient world around Israel, many cultures worshiped storm deities. The Canaanites worshiped Baal, the Babylonians worshiped Marduk, and the Assyrians worshiped Asshur. In Psalm 29, David takes this storm imagery and applies it to the Lord. He argues that thunderstorms demonstrate the Lord's power and should not be attributed to Baal or any other god.

The psalm begins with a call to all heavenly beings to "ascribe to the LORD glory and strength" (v. 1). The heart of the psalm is structured around seven statements David makes about the "voice of the LORD" (vv. 3–9). He pictures the Lord's voice thundering over the waters, breaking the mighty cedars of Lebanon, shaking the desert, and stripping the forests of their leaves. The imagery is mighty. God's power is untamable and demands respect.

Because of the Lord's power, the final two verses describe the Lord taking up His throne and reigning as King forever (vv. 10–11). Despite the Lord's destructive power celebrated in this psalm, the poem ends with the line, "the LORD blesses his people with peace" (v. 11). He uses His power to bring wholeness and well-being to His people. The voice of the Lord is ultimately the voice of peace for those who acknowledge and submit to His reign. Today, let's remember that "Holy, holy, holy is the LORD Almighty" (Isa. 6:3).

Go Deeper

Do we sometimes take our relationship with God too casually? How long has it been since you were overwhelmed by God's greatness and glory?

Pray with Us

"Holy, holy, holy" are you God! We come before You humbly, so overwhelmed by who You are. You are powerful. You are mighty. You hold all things in Your hands. Nothing escapes You. Nothing is beyond Your control. What a privilege to speak to the Almighty! Amen.

BOOK 1

PSALM 30

Praise Is Life

You turned my wailing into dancing; you removed my sackcloth and clothed me with joy.

PSALM 30:11

In the early 1970s, Charles Colson rose to power as Special Counsel to the President of the United States. But that came crashing down when he was indicted in the Watergate scandal. After coming to faith in Christ, Colson plead guilty and was sentenced to prison. Of that experience, he wrote, "My greatest humiliation—being sent to prison—was the beginning of God's greatest use of my life; He chose the one thing in which I could not glory for His glory."[16]

David's life followed a similar pattern. In Psalm 30, David recounts a time when he found himself in significant distress. He described being in the "realm of the dead" and on his way down "to the pit" (v. 3). Most commentators believe he experienced a serious illness. Upon reflection, David realized his downfall was due to his arrogance. Pride had been his downfall. He cried out to the Lord for mercy, and the Lord answered his prayer (v. 2).

What is most interesting in this psalm is one of the reasons David asked God to heal him. He told the Lord, "What is gained if I am silenced, if I go down to the pit? Will the dust praise you?" (v. 9). For David, life and death were more than just physical states. To be truly alive meant to live in right relation to God, and praising God. Death is described as a state where there is no longer any praise. David was overjoyed at the Lord's answered prayer. The Lord turned his "wailing into dancing" so that "my heart may sing your praises and not be silent. Lord my God, I will praise you forever" (vv. 11–12). Often when the Lord answers our prayers, it can be easy to forget the situation we were in. David models the importance of giving public testimony to the Lord's work in our life.

Go Deeper

Has the Lord answered your prayer recently? Let that be known. You'll give God the glory and can be a great encouragement to others.

Pray with Us

Lord, thank You for the many times You have turned our wailing into dancing. Thank You for answered prayers that bolster our faith and give us strength and courage for the future. We give You the concerns of our hearts today, knowing that You hear, and You can act! Amen.

BOOK 1

PSALM 31

Our Refuge

But I trust in you, LORD; I say, "You are my God."

PSALM 31:14

We all need a safe place where we can escape the fears and anxieties of the world. Young children who enter a new and intimidating situation will often hide behind their parent and grab onto their leg. Their parent is their safe place, or refuge. As adults, we choose different things to help feel secure. Our home or a favorite hobby can become a place of refuge.

Psalm 31 has two main movements. The first eighteen verses contain a prayer of trust and petition. The second half celebrates an answer to that prayer. In the first section, the themes of trust in God are interwoven with desperate cries for help. David looks to God as his safe place, or his refuge. "In you, LORD, I have taken refuge . . . be my rock of refuge, a strong fortress to save me" (vv. 1–2). David found the Lord to be faithful and declared his steadfast trust in Him (v. 5). Because of this deep level of trust, David is able to beg God for help. Here, he shouted commands at God: "Turn your ear to me, come quickly . . . deliver me . . . save me" (vv. 2, 15–16). David was the object of slander from enemies who wanted to take his life (vv. 11, 13, 17–18). That kind of public humiliation coupled with the threat of violence made David run to the Lord as his refuge.

The tone of the psalm changes dramatically in verses 19–24. David's prayer has been heard. The Lord is his secure refuge. David declares, "In the shelter of your presence you hide them from all human intrigues" (v. 20). This deliverance motivates David to call all of God's people to praise the Lord: "Be strong and take heart, all you who hope in the Lord" (v. 24).

Go Deeper
How do you respond when confronted by evil? What does it mean to take refuge in the Lord?

Pray with Us
Some days life feels desperate, God. It is easy to flail around in despair, wondering how we will survive. Like the psalmist we pray, "Turn your ear to me, come quickly . . . deliver me . . . save me" (vv. 2, 15–16). In the shelter of Your presence we find comfort and hope. Amen.

BOOK 1

PSALM 32

The Blessed One

> *Blessed is the one whose transgressions are forgiven, whose sins are covered.*
> PSALM 32:1

A Harvard study followed the lives of individuals including their triumphs and failures. Researchers concluded, "The surprising finding is that our relationships and how happy we are in our relationships have a powerful influence on our health."[17]

In Psalm 32, David highlights the importance of our relationship with God as a key to happiness. He declares "blessed" or "happy" those whose "transgressions are forgiven" (v. 1). David uses three different Hebrew words for sin, here translated as "transgressions . . . sins . . . sin" (vv. 1–2). The first term reflects intentional, or high-handed sin. The second word is the most general term for wrongdoing either intentional or unintentional. The third term references the guilt associated with sin (v. 2).

These three terms for sin are matched by three metaphors for forgiveness. The verb *forgiven* literally means "to carry" (v. 1). That is, our sin is like a burden we cannot bear. Someone must carry it for us. Second, David declares blessed the person whose sins are "covered" (v. 1). Finally, sin is pictured as a debt that is canceled (v. 2). In sum, the blessed person is not the one who never sins.

Rather, they are the kind of person who has sinned, but whose burden of that sin has been carried off by God.

In verses 3–5, David recounts a time when he tried to hide his sin. This led to a crushing sense of guilt and shame (v. 4). Finally, he confessed his sin to God and received forgiveness and relief (v. 5). He instructed others to follow his example. Joy and peace are to be found in the confession of sin and receiving of forgiveness.

Go Deeper

Do you have unconfessed sin? First Peter 2:24 tells us, "He [Jesus] bore our sins in his body on the cross." If you confess your sin to God, He is faithful to forgive because Jesus paid our debt.

Pray with Us

We come to You, God, today, to confess our sins. We have failed. We recognize the wrongfulness of our actions and our thoughts. We confess words spoken that should never have been said. We ask for Your mercy. Thank You for Your forgiveness. Amen.

PSALM 33

A Singing Faith

May your unfailing love be with us, LORD, even as we put our hope in you.
PSALM 33:22

One of the most effective ways that truth about God is taught is through singing. As one writer put it, "Christian hymnody contains some of the most tightly packed, concise doctrinal and devotional thought of the church. Through congregational song God's people learn their language about God; God's people learn how to speak with God. Songs of worship shape faith."[18]

In Psalm 33, the author rouses the people of God to "Sing joyfully to the LORD.... Sing to him a new song; play skillfully, and shout for joy" (vv. 1, 3). God is worthy of our best efforts to declare His goodness through musical artistry. This poem does what it commands. It teaches and celebrates several important truths about God.

God's Word is our standard for justice and truth (v. 4). It is one of God's most precious gifts. God is also the Creator of the universe. He spoke and the galaxies spun into existence (v. 6). The powerful seas and oceans are under His sovereign rule (v. 7). All the wonders of the universe burst into being at God's command (v. 9).

God is also sovereign over the nations (v. 10). Often this truth does not look obvious. When we look out at the world and see people and nations who are engaged in evil and destruction, we might wonder if God knows or cares about it. This psalm affirms that He "looks down and sees all mankind. . . . [He] considers everything they do" (vv. 13, 15). The response of faith is to "wait in hope for the LORD" (v. 20). The God who created the universe can be trusted to care for us and to administer justice, even if we might not see that fully implemented until the return of the Lord Jesus. At that time, all things will be made new (Rev. 21:5). Until then, we will continue to sing in hope.

Go Deeper

What are some of your favorite worship songs? How have they shaped your view of God? Do you know where those songs are rooted in Scripture?

Pray with Us

We long for Your return, Lord Jesus. Until that day, keep us singing Your praises! Music is Your gift to us, Lord. It is a way to testify to others and to worship You. May our voices reflect the hope in our hearts that is anchored on the promise of Your return. Amen.

BOOK 1

> PSALM 34

Taste and See

> *Taste and see that the LORD is good; blessed is the one who takes refuge in him.*
>
> PSALM 34:8

"Out of the frying pan and into the fire" describes the experience of getting out of one difficult situation only to land in another. In 1 Samuel 21, David was on the run from King Saul. He went to the last place anyone would expect to find him, the Philistine city of Gath. However, officials there identified him as David, the man who had killed thousands of Philistines in battle. In response, David feigned insanity and was able to get away. Reflecting upon that experience, David wrote Psalm 34.

In 1 Samuel 21, it looks like David got out of a difficult situation using only his wits and acting skills. However, David knew better. He confessed, "I sought the LORD, and he answered me. . . . This poor man called, and the LORD heard him" (vv. 4, 6). He understood that his rescue was the result of answered prayer. This psalm illustrates the truth that there is no contradiction between faithfully using our talents and skills and being fully reliant upon the Lord. In a difficult situation, David prayed to the Lord and tried to work out a plan for escape. Upon his deliverance, he recognized that the Lord should get the credit.

After this remarkable answer to prayer David urged others to trust in the Lord. Verses 8–14 contain ten imperatives calling the congregation to "taste and see . . . come and listen" (vv. 8, 11). He encourages the faithful to "fear the LORD" (v. 9), to trust fully in Him. Having a proper fear of the Lord calms our hearts from other fears (v. 4). It is important to note that having a proper fear of the Lord does not make us immune to trouble (v. 19). But it does mean we can trust that God is with us and hears our prayers.

Go Deeper
What is your first response to a difficult situation? What does the psalmist encourage us to do instead?

Pray with Us
We are prone to panic, Lord. Even when we have seen Your hand work in our lives during past troubles, we look to our current situation and forget to turn to You. Remind us, Lord. Remind us of what You have done in the past and help us trust You with today's situation. Amen.

BOOK 1

PSALM 35

God of Justice

My whole being will exclaim, "Who is like you, LORD?
You rescue the poor from those too strong for them, the poor and the needy
from those who rob them."

PSALM 35:10

At least one of the reasons why superhero movies are so popular is because by the end of story, the bad guys get caught, publicly denounced, and punished for their nefarious deeds. Batman always catches the Joker, and Superman gets his Lex Luthor.

We all have a longing for justice. In Psalm 35, David has been falsely accused. His enemies are people who have attacked him without reason (v. 7). David laments, "They slandered me without ceasing. Like the ungodly they maliciously mocked; they gnashed their teeth at me" (vv. 15–16).

The actions of these men were a deep betrayal. David had once been their friends and companions. When they suffered, David says, "I went about mourning as though for my friend or brother" (v. 14). He had treated them like family, prayed for them, and sought their good (vv. 11–14). But they paid him back through slandering, gossip, and inciting violence against him. They were causing chaos, not just for David, but for the whole community of Israel.

David prayed that the Lord would prevent them from carrying

out their evil plans. His petition is rooted in the character of God, "Who is like you, LORD? You rescue the poor from those too strong for them, the poor and needy from those who rob them" (v. 10). David prayed that God would act in accordance with His nature and administer justice for the vulnerable.

The vivid description of the wicked in this psalm provides an example for us to avoid. We should not betray friends, falsely accuse, or exploit others. Instead, in a world filled with injustice, we can pray that the Lord will see and take action (vv. 22–23).

Jesus knows what it meant to be falsely accused (John 15:25). God vindicated Jesus through His resurrection. In the same way, we can hope with confidence that God will one day make all wrongs right. It is appropriate for us to pray His justice to reign.

Go Deeper

Have you ever been the victim of injustice? How might this psalm help you process through that?

Pray with Us

God, we understand those feelings of hurt, betrayal, and anger. We live in a world where injustice seems to go on unchecked. Remind us that You will bring justice in the end and that You see all things. Go before us and defend us. We trust in You. Amen.

BOOK 1

> PSALM 36

Be Not Proud

Your love, LORD, reaches to the heavens, your faithfulness to the skies.

PSALM 36:5

In his masterpiece *Mere Christianity*, C. S. Lewis wrote perceptively about pride. "As long as you are proud you cannot know God. A proud man is always looking down on things and people: and, of course, as long as you are looking down, you cannot see something that is above you."[19]

In a similar way, the wicked have a skewed view of themselves and of God. The Psalms often paint a contrasting portrait of the righteous and the wicked. The main difference is not that one is sinless and the other sinful. In fact, the righteous often openly confess their sin to God. Rather, the main distinction between the two is that the righteous fear God and recognize their dependence upon Him; the wicked do not.

Psalm 36 focuses on the contrast between the wicked and God. Because the wicked do not fear God, they look to themselves as the most important reality in the universe. This leads them to flatter and deceive themselves (vv. 2–3). Their willful self-deception results in failure to "act wisely or do good" (v. 3). Instead, they become busy plotting and scheming against others (v. 4).

In marked contrast, the Lord's attributes of love, faithfulness, righteousness, and justice are celebrated (vv. 5–6). They are as important and as impressive as the "heavens," "skies," "highest mountains," and "great deep" (vv. 5–6). Instead of plotting the destruction of others, the Lord preserves "both people and animals" (v. 6). The Lord provides food, shelter, and protection to all who take refuge in Him (v. 7). The proper response to the Lord's remarkable care and provision is one of humility, gratitude, and trust. This sense of dependence on God is beautifully stated in verse 9: "For with you is the fountain of life; in your light we see light."

Go Deeper

Does it bother you to see the wicked prosper and the righteous suffer? Psalm 36 encourages us to focus instead on the greatness of God. How does that refocus our heart?

Pray with Us

Dear Lord, Thank You for Your love that "reaches to the heavens, your faithfulness to the skies" (Ps. 36:5). We place our trust and hope in You alone. Help us not to obsess about the wicked, but instead turn our attention to You. Amen.

BOOK 1

PSALM 37

Finding Significance

Better the little that the righteous have than the wealth of many wicked.

PSALM 37:16

After experiencing a crushing political defeat and breaking off an engagement to be married in 1841, Abraham Lincoln was in a dark place. He later talked about how he had contemplated suicide but refrained because he "had done nothing to make any human being remember that he had lived."[20] His desire to do something of lasting significance gave him the motivation he needed to persevere through difficult times.

In Psalm 37, David instructs us on how to have a life of lasting significance. He encourages the reader to "Trust in the LORD and do good.... Take delight in the LORD.... Be still before the LORD and wait patiently for him" (vv. 3, 4, 7). Trusting in the Lord means knowing and obeying the word of God. As David puts it, "The law of their God is in their hearts" (v. 31). We are to embrace a life of obedience (v. 27). If we do, the Lord will uphold us and our "inheritance will endure forever" (v. 18).

By contrast, the wicked are in a perilous position. It may look like they are flourishing and succeeding in life, but "like the grass they will soon wither" (v. 2). The wicked plot against those who follow God and oppress the poor and vulnerable (vv. 12, 14). They will not escape justice: "The LORD laughs at the wicked, for he knows their day is coming" (v. 13).

David is very honest about the struggle we feel when what we see in the world around us doesn't match up with what we believe. It may look to us like the wicked are winning. However, David tells us not to be anxious about their momentary success. We are to wait patiently for God to act at the right time and in the right way.

Go Deeper

Do you desire to live a life that has lasting significance? What kind of legacy do you want to leave behind?

Pray with Us

Too often this world disappoints us, God. We react with dismay even though You have told us that this world is not our home. Remind us to turn our focus heavenward! Help us not to be anxious, but to trust that Your plans will be accomplished. Your kingdom come! Amen.

BOOK 1

> PSALM 38

Suffering and Sin

Lord, do not forsake me; do not be far from me, my God. Come quickly to help me, my Lord and my Savior.

PSALM 38:21–22

When Adam and Eve sinned against God, their natural response was to hide (Gen. 3:7). They did not want to face God and the consequences of their actions. How often do we do the same thing! We try to cover up our sin and hide it from others. We might even think that somehow, we can hide it from God. Psalm 38 shows us what to do instead.

David provides us with a different model. He is suffering greatly and burdened by guilt (v. 4). His body is also wracked by pain: "My back is filled with searing pain; there is no heath in my body." (v. 7). David is under no illusion as to the source of his pain and guilt. He has sinned, and he is under God's judgment (vv. 1–4).

The Bible is clear that not all sickness or suffering is caused by a person's sin (e.g., Job). But in this case, David knows that his own sin is at the root of his maladies. Rather than trying to hide his sin, explain it away, or give excuses, David forthrightly confesses his wrongdoing (v. 18). Even though he is under God's judgment, he does not get angry at God or seek to run away from Him. Instead, he turns to God, openly confesses his sin, and begs for God to not abandon him (vv. 21–22). He is suffering under the hand of God and knows that his only help can come from the same source.

God not only judges sin, but he also provides deliverance from it. Jesus came to die for our sin so that we can be free and forgiven. When we do sin, we can follow the same pattern of confession that David shows us in this psalm, "If we confess our sins, he is faithful and just and will forgive us our sins and purify us from all unrighteousness" (1 John 1:9).

Go Deeper

Is it difficult for you to be open with God when you have sinned? How are some ways that this psalm could serve as a model for you?

Pray with Us

We come before You, God, as sinners. We confess that too often we choose the wrong way. We act to fulfill our own will, not considering Yours. We are deeply thankful that You gave Your Son, Jesus, so the penalty of our sins might be paid in full. Amen.

BOOK 1

PSALM 39

Life Is Short

> *"Show me, Lord, my life's end and the number of my days; let me know how fleeting my life is."*
>
> PSALM 39:4

Would it be better to win a silver medal or a bronze? In 1995, psychologists from Cornell University studied the reaction of Olympic silver and bronze medalists. They found that bronze medalists were significantly happier with their achievement than silver medalists. The reason is that silver medalists compared themselves with those who won gold, while the bronze medalists were happy to have a medal at all.

In Psalm 39, David is desperately trying to find the right perspective on life. He was in the middle of a challenging situation. He was suffering because of sin (vv. 8, 11). In addition, he was surrounded by wicked people (v. 1). So, after a sustained period of silence, David embraced two realizations that helped him gain a glimmer of hope.

First, David realizes that life is short. He says, "You have made my days a mere handbreadth" (v. 5). A handbreadth in ancient Israel was the width of four fingers, the smallest measurement available. He then shifts the image to compare life to a vapor or breath (v. 5). In language foreshadowing Ecclesiastes, he describes how the pursuit of wealth and brevity of life are meaningless (v. 6). David

99

realizes that what matters most is his relationship to the Lord, "But now, Lord, what do I look for? My hope is in you" (v. 7).

Second, David realizes that his sin has estranged him from God. "I dwell with you as a foreigner, a stranger, as all my ancestors were" (v. 12). He mourns deeply over his sin and longs for God to hear his cry. While this psalm does not come to a full resolution of these difficulties, David is well on his way toward restoration.

Go Deeper

Today, why not make a spiritual bucket list? How is God calling you to participate in His grand story? Be as specific as possible.

Pray with Us

With the psalmist we pray, "Show me, Lord, my life's end and the number of my days; let me know how fleeting my life is" (39:4). Teach us to value each moment and to make each day count for You, God! Amen.

BOOK 1

> PSALM 40

Giving Thanks

He put a new song in my mouth, a hymn of praise to our God.
Many will see and fear the LORD and put their trust in him.

PSALM 40:3

Before church on Sunday mornings, a small group of us meet to share prayer requests and praises. It always seems easier to remember prayer requests than it does reasons for thanksgiving. We don't have to search long to remember illness, financial needs, or plight of a wayward child. However, when it comes time for giving thanks, it often feels more difficult. Thanksgiving is not as readily on our lips.

In Psalm 40, David is not shy about giving thanks to the Lord. He remembers a time when the Lord heard his cry for help and answered (v. 1). He recounts, "He lifted me out of the slimy pit, out of the mud and mire; he set my feet on a rock and gave me a firm place to stand" (v. 2). This experience of deliverance led David to praise God publicly to let everyone know what God had done (v. 3).

David's personal experience of thanksgiving led him to recount God's attributes and character. He confessed that God is not primarily pleased by external obedience, but by obedience that comes from the heart (vv. 6–8). When we worship, our motives matter. It is the combination of sacrifice with the right attitude that makes it valuable (see Jer. 6:20; Amos 5:22). David resolved to not conceal who God is or what he has done. Instead, he will spend his days proclaiming God's faithful love to all (v. 10).

David's ability to look back and remember God's faithfulness gave him confidence to approach God afresh when a new set of difficulties had arisen (vv. 11–17). Following the Lord does not mean a life free from troubles or difficulties. In fact, just as we get delivered from one situation, it often feels like we end up in another one. David here reminds us to continue to come to him with our needs and to proclaim His faithfulness when those needs are met. On this side of the cross, we can always give thanks for the salvation that the Lord Jesus has achieved for us (1 John 2:1–2).

Go Deeper
Over and over in the Psalms we saw David get into trouble, plead for help, be rescued, and then get into difficulty again. His cycle is familiar to us. What can we learn from David's experience?

Pray with Us
Dear God, today we are focused on praise. We have so many reasons to thank You. As we reflect on all that You have given, we are deeply grateful. How great is our God! And how many reasons we have to give you thanks! Amen.

BOOK 1

PSALM 41

How to Be Like God

Blessed are those who have regard for the weak; the LORD delivers them in times of trouble.

PSALM 41:1

It seems natural for us to treat the wealthy, powerful, or beautiful with respect and deference. This can be seen in a host of ways from literally rolling out the red carpet at award ceremonies to the more subtle forms of attention at social gatherings. This dynamic can even be present at church. In the New Testament, James reminded the church, "If you show special attention to the man wearing fine clothes and say, 'Here's a good seat for you,' but say to the poor man, 'You stand there' or 'Sit on the floor by my feet,' have you not discriminated among yourselves and become judges with evil thoughts?" (James 2:3–4).

In Psalm 41, David pronounces a blessing on those who show regard to the weak and the vulnerable (v. 1). The reason why these people are blessed is because they are acting like their heavenly Father (vv. 2–3). This truth was driven home to David because he had been one of the weak. When he was sick, many people took the opportunity to slander him and treat him callously (vv. 5–8). His weak state revealed to him the truth about some of his so-called friends: "Even my close friend, someone I trusted, one who shared my bread, has turned against me" (v. 9). David condemns their actions because that is not how God treats the weak and the poor (vv. 1–3).

We live in a world wracked by sin. It is a world in which the poor, weak, and vulnerable often suffer the most. The New Testament reminds us that the Lord Jesus was not immune to this kind of treatment. He also was beaten, shamed, and betrayed by a friend (John 13:18). The God we worship knows what it is like to suffer. We also know that suffering is not the end. God, in His mercy, has promised that one day all things will be made new (Rev. 21:1). Until that day comes, we can hope in His mercy and try to live like Him (v. 10).

Go Deeper

How do we sometimes give extra respect to those society deems "important"? Are there people in your life that God is calling you to have mercy and compassion on?

Pray with Us

Dear Lord, we confess that sometimes we give special treatment and attention based on external attributes. It is easy to look up to the wealthy or powerful. But You came to us as someone marked by humility. Teach us Your ways, Lord. Amen.

BOOK 2
PSALMS 42–72

BOOK 2

PSALM 42

Longing for God

Why, my soul, are you downcast? Why so disturbed within me?
Put your hope in God, for I will yet praise him, my Savior and my God.

PSALM 42:5

A healthy human can live for weeks without food, but only for days without water. Water is essential for life. This is especially noticeable in arid climates like much of Israel. The psalm opens with the vivid metaphor, "As the deer pants for streams of water, so my soul pants for you, my God" (v. 1). Just as a deer in the wilderness would die without water, the psalmist desperately desires to meet with God.

This longing is particularly striking because the psalmist is going through some difficult trials. He is surrounded by enemies who taunt him, asking, "Where is your God?" (v. 3). He is in agony, his day and night marked by tears (vv. 3, 10). His spirit has become downcast and unsettled (v. 11). Yet, in this situation he does not say that he longs for deliverance from his enemies or relief from his pain. Instead, he longs for God.

The most difficult part of his suffering is that it seems as if God has turned his back on him. "All your waves and breakers have swept over me," he laments (v. 7). Yet amid his suffering, he recalls when times were better (v. 4). He regularly reminds himself to "put your hope in God, for I will yet praise him, my Savior and my God" (vv. 5, 11).

The good news is that our longing for God can be satisfied. The Lord Jesus proclaimed, "Let anyone who is thirsty come to me and drink" (John 7:37). He is the living water who can truly satisfy us with His presence and care (John 7:38). Even more, Christians are filled with the Holy Spirit, making us "the temple of the living God" (2 Cor. 6:16). Instead of longing for a physical temple to experience God's presence, we can remember that God sent his Spirit to dwell within us. When God seems far away, pour out your heart to God and know that He cares.

Go Deeper

How is our longing for God similar to being thirsty? In what ways does God satisfy that thirst?

Pray with Us

O God, there are days we feel like that parched deer, thirsting for just one drink. We are overcome by the worries and sorrow of this world. How good it is that we can turn to You. Only in You do we find refreshment. Thank You for Your care for us. Amen.

BOOK 2

> PSALM 43

Hope in Lament

Then I will go to the altar of God, to God, my joy and my delight.
I will praise you with the lyre, O God, my God.

PSALM 43:4

Psalms 42 and 43 were originally one psalm. This is evidenced in several manuscripts, as well as in the repeated refrain found in Psalms 42:5, 11 and 43:5. This psalm of lament is unique in that the psalmist does not simply pray for relief or beg God to help—although he does that as well (v. 1). Here he goes beyond a normal lament and speaks to himself. He tries to give himself advice on how to respond to his trouble.

"Why, my soul, are you downcast? Why so disturbed within me? Put your hope in God, for I will yet praise him, my Savior and my God" (v. 5). The psalmist asks some reflective questions. Sometimes we are not sure why we feel the way we do. Like the psalmist, we may be going through a difficult time. He realizes that he has fallen prey to the "deceitful and wicked" (v. 1). But that should not be enough to cause him to despair. He challenges himself to remember the hope that he has in God (v. 5). He needs to embrace God's promised future. Ultimately, God will work things out.

The psalmist asks God to lead him by "your light and your faithful care" (v. 3). The word "faithful care" points to the covenant God made with Israel. He points to God's promises in Scripture. The word "light" could also be a reference to God's Word (Ps. 119:105). God's Word should shape and guide our response to the world. Our hope is not found in our current circumstances but in the character and promises of a faithful God.

The psalmist ends this lament with a reminder that he will one day praise God again (v. 11). Biblical faith is characterized by hope. Just like the psalmist looked forward to the coming of the Messiah, we long for Christ's return. While lament may be the dominate note we experience in our lifetime, we know that praise will get the final word—"Hallelujah! For our Lord God Almighty reigns. Let us rejoice and be glad and give him glory! For the wedding of the Lamb has come" (Rev. 19:6–7). "Amen. Come, Lord Jesus" (Rev. 22:20).

Go Deeper

What are some promises in Scripture that help give you hope through trials? How does the hope of Christ's return shape your own lament?

Pray with Us

Dear Lord, how eagerly we wait for Your return. While we are on this earth, there is so much sorrow. There are so many worries. But in You, we have hope. The future You have promised gives us strength to face each day. Amen.

BOOK 2

PSALM 44

Awake, Lord!

Who shall separate us from the love of Christ? Shall trouble or hardship or persecution or famine or nakedness or danger or sword?

ROMANS 8:35

A prominent New Testament scholar walked away from his faith in God. He described his reason for abandoning faith in this way, "It was the problem of suffering that had created these doubts and that eventually led me to doubt it so much that I simply no longer believed it. If God helps his people—why doesn't he help his people? If he answers prayer, why doesn't he answer prayer?"[21] These are the same kinds of questions the psalmist raises in Psalm 45, but instead of driving him away from God, they drove him to engage more deeply with Him.

We do not know the exact circumstance in which Psalm 44 was written, but clearly, Israel had suffered a devastating military defeat. Reeling from the loss, the psalmist begins by recounting what God had done for Israel in the past. He had defeated other nations, especially during the time of Joshua (vv. 1–8). These victories were not accomplished because of the strength of Israel's army, but because God gave them victory (vv. 6–7).

Verse 9 describes Israel's current plight. They had been rejected and humbled by God. They had fled before their enemies (v. 10).

They had been plundered (v. 11). Worst of all, they had been publicly shamed and disgraced (vv. 13–16). Yet, this defeat was not for any known sin. Israel had not worshiped other gods or forgotten their covenant (vv. 17–21).

Israel thought that if they were faithful to God, God would be faithful to them. They could not understand their current defeat. Their theology did not align with their experience. This did not lead Israel to unbelief, but to their knees. They conclude by begging God to "Awake! . . . Rouse yourself! . . . Rise up and help us!" (vv. 23–26). In many ways, their request to God is not for an explanation, but for His action. Like the psalmist, we can express our bewilderment to God and plead for Him to act. We can cling to God when life doesn't make sense. Paul quotes this psalm, reminding believers that nothing, not even suffering, can separate us from the love of Christ (Rom. 8:35–39).

Go Deeper

Why is it tempting to feel abandoned by God during difficult trials? What does this psalm and Romans 8:35–39 teach us about God's faithfulness?

Pray with Us

God, we ask for your encouragement today. May Paul's quote from Psalm 44 encourage us even more. "Who shall separate us from the love of Christ?" (Rom. 8:35). We know the answer: Nobody! Amen.

BOOK 2

> PSALM 45

Future Hope

Your throne, O God, will last for ever and ever.

PSALM 45:6

The Battle of Gettysburg was costly. In just three days of fighting, there were more than 50,000 casualties. The nation was weary of war and wondered if it would ever end. In his famous Gettysburg Address, Abraham Lincoln presented a vision for the future: "That this nation, under God, shall have a new birth of freedom—and that government of the people, by the people, for the people shall not perish from the earth."

Psalms 42–44 present us with two main problems: separation from God's presence and military defeat. Psalms 45–49 provide answers to these problems. While Psalm 44 lamented a great military defeat, Psalm 45 presents a vision of a Davidic king who would "ride forth victoriously" and defeat the nations (vv. 4–5). This king is described in lofty terms: "Your throne, O God, will last for ever and ever" (v. 6). This description goes beyond any historical king of Israel and is a vision of a future Messiah.

While Psalms 42–43 lamented being cut off from God's presence (42:1–3; 43:3–4), Psalm 45 describes a bride being led into the presence of this exulted king "with joy and gladness" (v. 15). This psalm looked to a time of future hope for God's people. The bride described here is a figurative representation of the speaker of Psalm 42–43, who longed to come into God's presence with joy (43:4). This fits with the regular Old Testament image of God's relationship with Israel as a marriage (Jer. 2:2; 31:32; Isa. 54:5; Hos. 2:16–20). As one commentator explains, "It is best to understand Psalm 45 as speaking figuratively about a wedding between the divine Messiah-King and His people."[22]

Go Deeper

As we look at the state of the world around us, it can be easy to get discouraged. How does this psalm encourage us about the future?

Pray with Us

Together, we reflect on our future hope, the wedding feast of the Lamb. We thank You, Lord, that even now Your promise from Revelation is true, that You are "making everything new" (Rev. 21:5). Amen.

BOOK 2

PSALM 46

A Mighty Fortress

God is our refuge and strength, an ever-present help in trouble.

PSALM 46:1

In October 1527, Martin Luther's life looked bleak. He had been hiding for years because of his commitment to salvation by faith alone. In August, the bubonic plague swept the area where he lived. It must have felt like the world was falling apart. In response to this situation, he took comfort in Psalm 46 and wrote the hymn "A Mighty Fortress Is Our God."

Psalm 46 presents two terrifying images. First, a natural disaster with the ground shaking and mountains tumbling into the turbulent seas (vv. 2–3). Second, we see the foreign nations in an uproar (v. 6). One can imagine vast armies surrounding Jerusalem and threatening its very existence. Yet in the midst of these chaotic and frightening circumstances, the psalmist was able to proclaim, "God is our refuge and strength, an ever-present help in trouble" (v. 1). Israel was able to take comfort not in a vast army, or strongly fortified city, but in the presence of a God who is able to help (v. 5).

In verses 8–9, the psalmist addresses the nations directly, inviting them to "come and see what the LORD has done" (v. 8). They are invited to remember the great victories He achieved in the past: the defeat of Pharaoh's army at the Red Sea, for example (v. 9). The tone shifts dramatically in verse 10. The Lord Himself addresses the rebellious and threatening nations. He commands them to "be still and know that I am God; I will be exalted among the nations" (v. 10). The command to "be still" is not so much an encouragement to silent meditation but a warning to cease fighting and to acknowledge the Lord's sovereignty.

Go Deeper

While terrifying and frightening things continue to happen in the world today, what can we depend upon? What solution does this psalm provide to our earthly trials?

Pray with Us

Are you going through difficulties right now? Read Psalm 46 back to the Lord as your prayer, and may its beautiful words strengthen you. Indeed, "God is our refuge and strength, an ever-present help in trouble" (Ps. 46:1).

BOOK 2

PSALM 47

Clap Your Hands

"And I, when I am lifted up from the earth, will draw all people to myself."
JOHN 12:32

C. S. Lewis noticed that when people find something they love, they naturally want other people to join them in praising it. "Isn't the painting beautiful?" "Wasn't that play magnificent?" He reflected upon the reason for this: "I think we delight to praise what we enjoy because the praise not merely expresses but completes the enjoyment; it is its appointed consummation."[23]

In today's psalm, the writer encourages all the nations to "Clap your hands . . . shout to God with cries of joy" (v. 1). He was so delighted in God that he wanted the whole world to join him. God had done great things for Israel. He had subdued the Canaanites under the leadership of Joshua during the period of the conquest (v. 3). He had fulfilled His promise to Abraham that Israel would dwell in the land of Canaan (v. 4). This demonstrated His love for Israel and His faithfulness to them (v. 4).

God is also to be praised because He is "awesome" (v. 2). He rules over the nations and is "greatly exalted" (vv. 8–9). This psalm envisions God ascending to His heavenly throne and ruling over all people (vv. 5–8). In a final picture of God's universal rule, the poet describes how "the nobles of the nations assemble as the people of the God of Abraham" (v. 9). Even though this psalm began by celebrating things God had specifically done to help Israel, it ends by presenting a vision of leaders from every nation assembling with Israel in homage to God. This anticipates the ultimate fulfillment of God's promise to Abraham that through his offspring "all peoples on earth will be blessed" (Gen. 12:3).

Go Deeper

How comfortable are you with telling others about your faith? One way to think about evangelism is wanting other people to join you in your delight in Jesus and what He has done for you.

Pray with Us

We invite you to pray and worship the Lord in a new way. Maybe follow the invitation in this psalm to "clap your hands" or to "shout to God with cries of joy" (v. 1). The Lord delights in our creativity!

BOOK 2

PSALM 48

Great Is Your Faithfulness

Great is the LORD, and most worthy of praise, in the city of our God, his holy mountain.

PSALM 48:1

When Hezekiah was king of Judah, the powerful nation of Assyria marched into their land and threatened Jerusalem. The commander of the Assyrians taunted the Judean king, even offering to give him two thousand horses for their upcoming battle (2 Kings 18:23). Hezekiah went into the temple and prayed for God to intervene. That night, the angel of the Lord decimated the Assyrian army, forcing them to head back to their own country (2 Kings 19:35–36).

This event had a profound impact on the nation of Judah. It is possible that Psalm 48 was written in response to this crisis and God's miraculous intervention. The psalmist proclaims, "Great is the LORD, and most worthy of praise" (v. 1). That sets the tone for this joyful hymn which celebrates Jerusalem as the place where God dwells as the "Great King" (v. 2). He compares Jerusalem to the "heights of Zaphon" (v. 2). Zaphon was the mountain north of Israel where Canaanites believed their god Baal reigned as king. The psalmist here declares that the Lord alone is the real King.

Julius Caesar once famously proclaimed, "Veni, Vidi, Vici" ("I came, I saw, I conquered"). The kings described in verses 4–7 "came, saw, and fled!" They surrounded Jerusalem but were dismayed by its secure position. The city was not secure because of its magnificent towers or fortifications, but because it was where God dwelled (v. 8). The psalmist ends by meditating on the faithfulness of God to protect His people (v. 9). Because of the salvation God has accomplished, the people praise Him "to the ends of the earth" (v. 10). His people want to pass on to their children and grandchildren their testimony of God's faithfulness.

Go Deeper

How can you tell the next generation about God's work your life? Consider one way you can share your faith stories with your children or grandchildren.

Pray with Us

Lord, our prayer is that each of us will leave a legacy of faith, telling the next generation about your love and mercy in our lives. May we have the strength and determination to serve you faithfully until the end.

BOOK 2

PSALM 49

Wealth and God

"For even the Son of Man did not come to be served, but to serve, and to give his life as a ransom for many."

MARK 10:45

Wellington R. Burt was a lumber baron in the late nineteenth century and one of the wealthiest men in America. While he was generous with others, he was famously tight-fisted with his own family. He included a "spite clause" in his will that specified that none of his descendants could inherit any of his money until twenty-one years after the death of his last grandchild. Sure enough, in 2010, his $100 million fortune was divided between his twelve great-great-great-grandchildren.[24]

Psalm 49 addresses prosperity and the wealthy. The "wicked" in verse 5 are people who "trust in their wealth" (v. 6). They find their value in what they have acquired and look down on those in a more humble position (vv. 6, 13). The psalmist points out that the wealthy are often praised in this life simply because they are wealthy (v. 18). Wealth seems to erase moral distinctions. These wealthy are honored and even had lands named after them (v. 11).

However, we do not have to fear these people or be envious of them (v. 5). Nothing they acquired will last in any significant sense: "Their tombs will remain their houses forever, their dwellings for endless generations" (v. 11). Their incredible wealth will not be enough to redeem their life from the grave (v. 7). Ultimately, their wealth will be left to others and they will be forgotten (v. 10). The psalmist is confident that "God will redeem me from the realm of the dead; he will surely take me to himself" (v. 15). He knows that death will not have the ultimate say for him because of his relationship with God. His hope is that he will live with God forever.

Go Deeper

What does the psalmist mean when he says that "no payment is ever enough" (v. 8)? How did Jesus solve this problem for us?

Pray with Us

Thank You, Lord, for Your gift of eternal life. We praise You for Your victory on the cross as You gave Your life "as a ransom for many" (Mark 10:45). In You we have hope, forgiveness, and a future. Amen.

BOOK 2

PSALM 50

Wrong Motives

"For every animal of the forest is mine, and the cattle on a thousand hills."
PSALM 50:10

Why do you pray? Read your Bible? Tithe? Do you do these things to earn God's favor? Today's psalm explores the difference between the things we do that truly honor God and the things we do which are a thinly disguised attempt to impress God with our own righteousness.

In most psalms, Israel addresses God. In today's reading, God addresses Israel. Verses 1–6 describe God summoning the heavens and the earth "that he may judge his people" (v. 4). God's message to Israel begins with a reminder. In the ancient world, people offered sacrifices in order to feed the gods. God makes clear that He does not need their sacrifices in order to satisfy His hunger (v. 12). He owns every animal of the forest and the "cattle on a thousand hills" (v. 10). Furthermore, God does not eat bulls or goats (v. 13).

Sacrifices were intended to teach Israel about the nature of sin and its atonement as well as to express thanks to God. However, the sacrificial system could easily be misunderstood. Israel could have thought that if they just did the right rituals and sacrificed the right offerings, then they would be acceptable. God strongly counters that idea. It is not enough to sacrifice in the right way—the motives of the worshiper matter. God accused some in Israel of stealing, false testimony, and adultery and then coming to sacrifice and reciting the law before God (vv. 16–21). This kind of worship is abhorrent to God, who warns, "Consider this, you who forget God, or I will tear you to pieces, with no one to rescue you" (v. 22). However, to those who honor Him in the right way, He promises, "I will show my salvation" (v. 23).

Go Deeper

How does your relationship with God impact all the areas of your life? Is it limited to Sunday morning? How can you resolve to follow faithfully for the rest of the week?

Pray with Us

Dear God, we know that our prayers and worship are not limited to Sunday. Help us be consistent and faithful in our walk with You every day. Thank You for Your grace and for the sustaining power of the Holy Spirit. Amen.

BOOK 2

> PSALM 51

True Repentance

Wash away all my iniquity and cleanse me from my sin.

PSALM 51:2

Seventeenth-century pastor John Donne was also a celebrated poet. In one of his *Holy Sonnets* reflecting on the second coming, he wrote, "When we are there; here on this lowly ground / Teach me how to repent; for that's as good / As if thou hadst seal'd my pardon with thy blood."[25] Donne understood the power of repentance.

Psalm 51 is one of the most famous chapters in the Psalter. For thousands of years, it has modeled for believers a prayer of repentance. The title of the psalm informs us that it was written after David had been confronted for committing adultery with Bathsheba (2 Sam. 12). David's sin included coveting a neighbor's wife, adultery, lying, and murder. He begins his prayer by pleading to God for mercy, "Have mercy on me, O God" (Ps. 51:1). He knows that he does not deserve God's forgiveness. His hope is in the compassion of God.

David clearly and honestly acknowledges his sin. He realizes that his sin comes from a deep place within him: "Surely I was sinful at birth, sinful from the time my mother conceived me" (v. 5). He prays for God not only to forgive him but also to cleanse him and restore him to a state of holiness (v. 7). He prays that God would so work in his heart that it would be transformed (v. 10). He wants to not just be forgiven but also changed. David's cry is the essence of repentance. Finally, David declares that in his restored state, he will engage in ministry. He will "teach transgressors your ways, so that sinners will turn back to you" (v. 13). He desires to use his new life to declare God's praise (v. 15).

Go Deeper
What is repentance? What can we learn from David's model of turning from sin?

Pray with Us
Our merciful Lord, we come before You boldly in a prayer of confession. Just as You mercifully forgave David's sin, we ask that You forgive ours today. Amen.

BOOK 2

PSALM 52

Destructive Words

The tongue has the power of life and death, and those who love it will eat its fruit.

PROVERBS 18:21

When David was fleeing from King Saul, he came to the sanctuary city of Nob and asked Ahimelek the priest for help. Ahimelek assumed David was still working for Saul and assisted him with provisions. One of Saul's servants, Doeg the Edomite, overheard this and denounced the priest to Saul, who ordered that Ahimelek and eighty-five other priests be put to death (1 Sam. 21:1–8; 22:6–19). Today's reading represents David's lament over this tragic turn of events.

David addresses Doeg directly in the opening of the psalm: "Why do you boast of evil, you mighty hero?" (v. 1). He denounces Doeg for his deceit. In a vivid image, David describes the deceitful tongue as a razor that brings destruction (v. 2). Words can do incredible damage. These destructive words come out of the heart of a person whose values are skewed. "You love evil rather than good, falsehood rather than speaking the truth" (v. 3).

In verses 5–7, David reminds his adversary that God is aware of what he has done and will bring judgment (v. 5). While it might look like the wicked prosper and the righteous suffer, that would not be the case forever. One day, "the righteous will see and fear; they will laugh at you, saying, 'Here now is the man who did not make God his stronghold'" (vv. 6–7). David contrasts himself with the wicked. Drawing from the image of the righteous as a flourishing tree in Psalm 1, David declares, "But I am like an olive tree flourishing in the house of God" (v. 8). Instead of putting his faith in his own achievements, David trusts in the Lord's "unfailing love" (v. 8). Instead of deceit, his lips will pour forth praise to God (v. 9).

Go Deeper

How can words affect our relationship with others? Our relationship with God? Ask the Lord to help you use the gift of language wisely today.

Pray with Us

Thank You, Lord, for the gift of language. We ask for wisdom to use it for good and not for evil. May we build up and encourage others and not destroy. Use our words to honor You, the Living Word! Amen.

BOOK 2

> PSALM 53

All Have Sinned

For all have sinned and fall short of the glory of God.
ROMANS 3:23

According to the Pew Research Center, around 28 percent of US adults are considered "religiously unaffiliated," people who describe themselves as atheists, agnostics, or nothing in particular.[26] This statistic should arouse our compassion. As Paul reminded the church in Ephesus, they too were once "without hope and without God in the world" (Eph. 2:12).

In today's reading David declares, "The fool says in his heart, 'There is no God'" (Ps. 53:1). David is not referring to a philosophical atheist—that kind of person did not likely exist in the ancient world. Rather, this "fool" is a functional atheist, people who live their lives as if God does not see or care. There are consequences to this kind of unbelief. The lack of a moral standard or sense of accountability leads to corrupt and destructive actions (v. 1).

Beginning in verse 2, we see God's view of humanity. The conclusion is sobering. "Everyone has turned away, all have become corrupt; there is no one who does good, not even one" (v. 3). It is not just a small percent who do not live up to God's standard, but all of humanity. Living as a functional atheist leads to a life filled with fear. David describes it this way: "There they are, overwhelmed with dread, where there was nothing to dread" (v. 5). Like people who run from shadows, the evildoers in this psalm live in fear and under God's judgment (v. 5). David expresses a longing for deliverance and salvation, "Oh, that salvation for Israel would come out of Zion!" (v. 6).

Go Deeper

Is it possible to earn your salvation? If not, then why does keeping the law matter? (See Romans 3:11–12 and 6:23.)

Pray with Us

Dear God, today's psalm is so convicting. Humanity is totally depraved apart from You. There is no one who is righteous. We praise You that You didn't leave us in this lost state and for salvation through Christ! Amen.

BOOK 2

PSALM 54

Crying for Help

Surely God is my help; the Lord is the one who sustains me.
PSALM 54:4

My children often come to me with requests that might seem strange if someone else asked them: "Can you read me a book? Can you make a sandwich for me? Can you play cars with me?" Yet, because I am their father, they know that they have the right to ask those kinds of things. That is often how David approached God. In the Psalms, David makes bold and specific requests of God because he has a relationship with Him.

David penned this lament after being betrayed by the Ziphites (1 Sam. 23:19–20). These were men from his own tribe. David addresses God urgently asking for salvation from the hand of these "arrogant foes" who were "people without regard for God" (v. 3), or more literally, men who "have not set God before them."

David is honest about his sense of betrayal. He expresses his desire for vengeance (v. 5). God invites us to be honest about our anger so we can hand over our desire for revenge to Him (Rom. 12:19). In spite of his imminent danger, David expresses confidence in God. He declares, "Surely God is my help; the Lord is the one who sustains me" (v. 4). His attitude stands in stark contrast to his enemies. His eyes look first to God for help. As one commentator put it, "Placing our gaze fully on God changes the way we see the rest of the world."[27] David ends this short lament with a vow. When God delivers him, he will not be silent about it (v. 6).

Go Deeper

When we are in difficult and trying circumstances, how can we fix our eyes on Jesus? Soak in the words of this classic hymn today: "Turn your eyes upon Jesus / Look full in His wonderful face / And the things of earth will grow strangely dim / In the light of His glory and grace."

Pray with Us

Following David's example in Psalm 54, we ask You, Lord, to help us grow in our trust and dependence on You. In any circumstance we face today or tomorrow, may our eyes look only to You first. Amen.

BOOK 2

PSALM 55

When Betrayed

Cast your cares on the Lord and he will sustain you;
he will never let the righteous be shaken.

PSALM 55:22

Stress and anxiety can take a toll on one's body. Doctors advise that emotional stress can cause dizziness, a fast heartbeat, the inability to concentrate, headaches, muscle tension, and even short-term memory loss. If not handled well, high emotional stress can have a lasting negative impact.

David was in a state of extreme stress. He had experienced persecution and danger (v. 3). His enemies prowled the streets looking for an opportunity to attack him (vv. 9–11). Most poignantly, one of his enemies had been at one time a close friend. He laments, "But it is you, a man like myself, my companion, my close friend with whom I once enjoyed sweet fellowship at the house of God" (vv. 13–14). This situation has taken a physical toll on David. "My heart is in anguish within me; the terrors of death have fallen on me. Fear and trembling have beset me; horror has overwhelmed me" (vv. 4–5).

David's first impulse was to run. "Oh, that I had the wings of a dove! I would fly away and be at rest" (v. 6). Perhaps you have been in a situation where your greatest desire was to flee. David's heart expressed not the courage of the man who had faced down giants but the timidity of a bird. His second impulse was to turn his anxiety over to God. Although David's circumstances looked grim, God has not changed (v. 19). He assured himself that God heard his cry for help (v. 17). He knew that God would ultimately judge the wicked (v. 23). This psalm was David's way of casting his cares on the Lord (v. 22).

Go Deeper

How does this psalm model prayer for us, especially when we feel betrayed? Remember that even our Lord Jesus was betrayed by a close friend and surrounded by enemies.

Pray with Us

Father God, we have been given a somber reminder of the pain of betrayal. We understand the anguish that David experienced as we sometimes feel that way too. Through Your power, help us heal, overcome, and forgive. Amen.

BOOK 2

> PSALM 56

When I Fear

When I am afraid, I put my trust in you. In God, whose word I praise.

PSALM 56:3-4

Moses experienced fear. When God called him to deliver Israel from Egypt, Moses was afraid that his own people would not listen to him, that Pharaoh would not respect him, and that he could not speak well enough to accomplish the job (Ex. 3–4). Even so, God worked through Moses. His fear was overcome by God's promise to be with him every step of the way.

In Psalm 56, David was fearful. He had enemies dogging his every step (vv. 1–2). They chased him "all day long" with the hope that they would ultimately take his life (vv. 2, 6). These adversaries wanted not only to kill David but also to destroy his reputation (v. 5).

David confessed that he was afraid (v. 3). This admission was the first step to transforming his mindset. "When I am afraid, I put my trust in you," he declared (v. 3). David reminded himself of two truths about God. First, God is powerful. He can take down nations and deliver us from any situation (vv. 7, 13). Second, David reminded himself that God cares for him. In a beautiful image, David declared, "You have kept count of my tossings; put my tears in your bottle. Are they not all in your book?" (v. 8 ESV). God not only knows about David's suffering, He keeps track of every sleepless night and every shed tear.

Having reminded himself of God's power and compassion, David was able to change his perspective. He proclaimed, "In God I trust and am not afraid. What can man do to me?" (v. 11). Humans can do enormous damage to one another, but David's point here was that they were not powerful enough to thwart God's plan for his life.

Go Deeper

Did you know that one of the most often repeated command in Scripture is "Do not be afraid"? How does this psalm encourage you to react to feelings of fear?

Pray with Us

"When I am afraid, I put my trust in you" (Ps. 56:3). These words show us how to escape the grip of fear, O God. We look to You in both good and bad times, in times of victory as well as failure. Amen.

BOOK 2

PSALM 57

Safe with You

Have mercy on me, my God, have mercy on me, for in you I take refuge.

PSALM 57:1

When our children were toddlers, and we brought them into an unfamiliar situation, like a wedding or graduation party, they would often hide behind my legs when someone tried to talk to them. When little ones feel uncomfortable, they look for safety by clinging to a parent.

In Psalm 57, David reflects on the time he had "fled from Saul into the cave." This could be the cave of Adullam (1 Sam. 22) or the cave in the Desert of Ein Gedi (1 Sam. 24). David prays, "Have mercy on me, my God, have mercy on me, for in you I take refuge" (Ps. 57:1). It would seem that the cave was his refuge. But David knew better. The Lord is a far more secure place to hide. David describes God as a mother bird who protects her young by spreading her wings (v. 1).

David was in a difficult situation. He describes his flight from Saul as being "in the midst of lions ... men whose teeth are spears and arrows, whose tongues are sharp swords" (v. 4). Yet in the midst of this violent onslaught, David expresses confidence in God's great love and faithfulness (v. 10). Even though David has not experienced deliverance *yet*, his confidence in God makes him want to break out in praise. "I will sing and make music, Awake, my soul! Awake, harp and lyre! I will awaken the dawn" (vv. 7–8). David wanted others to join him in this praise. He called out to other nations and peoples to hear about the glory of God (v. 9). In a world where each nation worshiped their own deities, David affirmed that the God of Israel is actually the God over all nations and peoples. His glory is over "all the earth" (v. 11).

Go Deeper

What are some current threats to your own safety and security? How can you learn to deal with these threats from David's model of lament as well as his expression of confidence in God's faithfulness?

Pray with Us

David was hiding in a cave, but he knew his real refuge was in You, God. May we too find our security, protection, and confidence in You and not in the things of this world. Amen.

BOOK 2

PSALM 58

Longing for Justice

"Surely the righteous still are rewarded; surely there is a God who judges the earth."

PSALM 58:11

Of the 3,500 species of snakes in the world, only about six hundred are venomous. Nevertheless, snakes can do significant damage. According to the World Health Organization, every year 81,410 to 137,880 people die from snake bites.[28] In today's reading, David compares his enemies to snakes and the damage they inflict—to venom.

In the opening of Psalm 58, David confronts corrupt rulers directly. The word here for "rulers" is unusual and could be a reference to supernatural beings or human judges. Based on the language of the psalm as a whole, it is best to understand the term as a reference to corrupt human rulers, who were encouraged and empowered by malevolent spiritual entities. These corrupt rulers had caused enormous suffering, violence, and injustice (v. 2).

Envisioning them as poisonous snakes, or ravenous lions, David asks God to "break the teeth in their mouths, O God; LORD, tear out the fangs of those lions!" (v. 6). David prays that these rulers would become powerless to continue their oppression. David is honest with God about his desire for their defeat. He prays that they will be "like a slug that melts away" or "like a stillborn child that never sees the sun" (v. 8). His harsh language may be difficult for modern readers, but it is important to remember two things. First, David is praying this to God. God already knows the deepest desires of our heart and can handle our unbridled honesty. By praying, we can give these desires over to God. Second, David's ultimate desire was for justice to be done, so that people will know that "there is a God who judges the earth" (v. 11).

Go Deeper

Are you personally suffering today? If not, consider praying for believers around the world who are suffering for their faith in Christ. Together we pray, "Amen. Come, Lord Jesus" (Rev. 22:20).

Pray with Us

Today, Lord, we pray for believers around the world who are suffering for their faith. They endure injustice and persecution, but You, the Lord of justice, the righteous Judge, are on their side. We praise You—Your truth will prevail! Amen.

BOOK 2

PSALM 59

A Broken World

But I will sing of your strength, in the morning I will sing of your love.

PSALM 59:16

Since Adam and Eve rebelled against God in the garden of Eden, the world has been broken. As one writer expressed, we live in a world where people "exhibit a corruption of thought, emotion, intention, speech, and disposition."[29] This impacts every area of our life: work, school recess, even a well-planned vacation. Things are not the way they were supposed to be.

Today's reading expresses the emotion of living in a broken world. David feels surrounded by adversaries who want to take him down. He describes them as enemies, attackers, evildoers, bloodthirsty, people who lie in wait, conspirators, and slanderers (vv. 1–5). He pictures them like vicious, wild dogs prowling the streets, waiting to pounce (vv. 6, 14). This psalm reminds us of how persistent and pervasive evil is in our world.

But Psalm 59 also reminds us of a deeper reality. God is David's strength and fortress (v. 1). David can call to God for deliverance knowing that He is able to hear and powerful enough to act (vv. 5, 8). While this psalm is full of the violence and scheming of the wicked, its final word returns our focus to God's love and faithfulness. "You, God, are my fortress, my God on whom I can rely"

(v. 17). The word translated "rely" is the Hebrew word for God's covenant love, *hesed*. God is love and will remain faithful to His promises. David knows this and even though his enemies "prowl about the city," he declares, "but I will sing of your strength, in the morning I will sing of your love" (vv. 14, 16).

Go Deeper

What examples do you see of this broken world? How can you turn this observation into a praise to our perfect and unchanging God?

Pray with Us

Like David, we live in a broken world. And like David, we cry out for Your mercy and justice, God. May the words of this psalm be our prayer today: "You, God, are my fortress, my God on whom I can rely" (Ps. 59:17). Amen.

BOOK 2

PSALM 60

The Promises of God

With God we will gain the victory.

PSALM 60:12

God makes many promises in the Bible. He promised Abraham that his descendants would be a numerous as the stars in the sky (Gen. 15:5). Jesus promised that those who seek first His kingdom would have their needs met (Matt. 6:33). Paul assured the Philippians that if they presented their requests to God, "the peace of God . . . will guard your hearts and minds" (Phil. 4:7). What do we do when our experience does not line up with what God has promised?

The people of Israel had been promised by God that the land of Canaan would be given to them (Gen. 12:7). In today's reading, Israel had suffered a military defeat. David states, "You have rejected us, God, and burst upon us; you have been angry—now restore us!" (Ps. 60:1). The promise of the land was under threat. What did David do? He clearly describes the problem to God. "You have shaken the land and torn it open. . . . You have shown your people desperate times" (vv. 2–3). Then in poetic language, David reminds God of His promise regarding the land: "God has spoken from his sanctuary: 'In triumph I will parcel out Shechem and measure off the Valley of Sukkoth'" (v. 6). David asks God for help: "Save us and help us with your right hand, that those you love may be delivered" (v. 5).

Finally, David restates his trust in God. He confesses that "human help is worthless" and "with God we will gain the victory, and he will trample down our enemies" (vv. 11–12). David knows that his temporary failure doesn't mean that God's promises had failed. He trusts that God will be able to make things right.

Go Deeper

How does Psalm 60 model for us how to relate to God in times when His promises seem unfulfilled?

Pray with Us

When we face disappointment, Lord—when our plans are uprooted—help us remember and cling to Your Word and place our trust in You alone. Help us stay faithful even in challenging times. Amen.

BOOK 2

PSALM 61

Hear My Cry

I long to dwell in your tent forever and take refuge in the shelter of your wings.

PSALM 61:4

During my years as a pastor, I had the privilege of visiting the sick in the hospital. I vividly remember one day meeting with an older man from our congregation who was nearing the end of his life. I asked if we could pray together. He began by praying the words of this psalm as if they were his own. "Hear my cry, O God; listen to my prayer. From the ends of the earth I call to you, I call as my heart grows faint" (vv. 1–2).

We do not know the precise situation David was in when he wrote this psalm, but he was clearly in distress. He felt far from God and longed to experience His presence and hand of blessing again. Throughout this poem, David uses rich metaphors to describe God. He calls God "the rock that is higher than I," a "refuge," and a "strong tower" (vv. 2–3). In a world filled with danger, being in God's presence is safer than any castle or stronghold.

In verse 4, David describes his desire to live in the tabernacle, where God's presence was most manifest in ancient Israel. He prays, "I long to dwell in your tent forever and take refuge in the shelter of your wings." Even in his distress, David is confident that God can hear him and that He cares (v. 5). For David, God was never more than a prayer away.

In verses 6–7, David prays for the king. He asks that God would protect him with his covenant love and faithfulness (v. 7). David understood that in his office as king, he represented both Israel as a nation and the future hope of a descendant on the throne forever (2 Sam. 7:11–16). This allows him to end his prayer on a note of hope and praise.

Go Deeper
How did David find hope, even in his distress? Do you share in that hope? Give thanks to God today.

Pray with Us
Lord, we thank You for the beautiful messianic prophecy of Psalm 61. David saw ahead, by the power of the Holy Spirit, to the coming of the Eternal King—the son of David, the son of Abraham (Matt. 1:1). Amen.

BOOK 2

PSALM 62

Rest in God

Yes, my soul, find rest in God; my hope comes from him.
PSALM 62:5

It is easy to say "I trust in God" when things are going well. However, when a crisis hits, our trust is put to the test. We may think that we trust God to supply all of our needs until we are faced with a lost job, or a sudden downturn in the economy. In that moment, we may find that we have really been trusting in wealth for our security.

In today's reading, David's position and security have come under threat. He feels as fragile as a "leaning wall" or a "tottering fence" ready to topple at any moment (v. 3). His enemies are particularly insidious in that they speak well of him to his face, but curse him in their hearts and spread lies about him to others (v. 4).

This situation has caused David to reevaluate what he puts his trust in. He declares that most of the things that people look to for security are not able to provide it. He says, "The lowborn are but a breath, the highborn are but a lie" (v. 9). In other words, your social position will not bring you security. Riches are a vain hope as well. Therefore, you should "not set your heart on them" (v. 10).

True contentment and security are gifts that come from God alone. "Truly my soul finds rest in God; my salvation comes from him" (v. 1). Therefore it only makes sense to "trust in him at all times, you people; pour out your hearts to him, for God is our refuge" (v. 8). David concludes the psalm by describing the two primary reasons why God is so trustworthy. He is the only source of true power (v. 11) and He is just (v. 12).

Go Deeper

What or who are you putting your trust in? Ask the Lord today to show you if there are any areas of your life that you need to reevaluate so that you can truly place your trust in God and find rest in Him alone.

Pray with Us

Lord, help us learn to rest in You. Help us overcome fear and anxiety with the peace that only You can bring. We make David's words our prayer today: "Truly my soul finds rest in God, my salvation comes from him" (Ps. 62:1). Amen.

BOOK 2

PSALM 63

Better than Life

*You, God, are my God, earnestly I seek you; I thirst for you,
my whole being longs for you.*

PSALM 63:1

The early church father Augustine of Hippo sought for meaning or fulfillment in his life for years. When he finally came to faith in Christ, he gave thanks to God by saying, "You have made us for yourself, and our heart is restless until it rests in you."[30]

In today's reading, David expresses a deep longing for God's presence. He knows that only God can satisfy. He confesses, "I thirst for you, my whole being longs for you, in a dry and parched land where there is no water" (v. 1). As a dry and cracked desert landscape needs water for life to flourish, David knows that he needs intimacy with God in order to survive.

David finds the answer by searching his memory. He looks back on the times when he saw God in the sanctuary and beheld His power and glory (v. 2). He remembers God's faithful commitment to His people. He declares, "Your love is better than life" (v. 3). The word for love here is *hesed*. It refers to God's loyalty to His covenant with Israel. David knows that to be in right relationship with God is more important than life itself.

As David is reminded of God's faithfulness, he breaks forth in praise: "I will praise you as long as I live, and in your name I will lift up my hands" (v. 4). David prayed this while in the wilderness. He was likely on the run from Saul, or Absalom. In that context, sleep is a time when one would be especially vulnerable to surprise or attack. David declares, "On my bed I remember you; I think of you through the watches of the night" (v. 6). He knows that God is his shelter. Because of this, he is confident in God's protection (vv. 9–10). He knows that ultimately the "mouths of liars will be silenced," but his mouth will be wide open "with singing lips" (vv. 11, 5).

Go Deeper

In Christ's work on the cross, we have seen God's love powerfully displayed. When we feel like God is distant, like we are in the wilderness, what should we remember?

Pray with Us

God, David praised You in "a dry and parched land"—the wilderness of Judah. May we too praise you when we walk through hard and lonely times. Lord, help us see that "your love is better than life" (Ps. 63:3). Amen.

BOOK 2

PSALM 64

The Hope of the Righteous

The fear of the LORD is the beginning of knowledge, but fools despise wisdom and instruction.

PROVERBS 1:7

What is the difference between the righteous and the wicked? Is it simply that the righteous generally do the right thing while the wicked do not? While that is partially true, it's not the full story. As seen in our study of the second book of Psalms, the primary difference between the righteous and the wicked relates to their understanding of God as a just judge. The righteous believe that God is just and that He will hold all people accountable for what they do. They live in a healthy fear of God. The wicked do not believe that God sees what they do, or that He cares.

In today's reading, David complains about his enemies, saying, "They encourage each other in evil plans, they talk about hiding their snares; they say, 'Who will see it?'" (v. 5). These enemies work together to slander David to try to bring him down. They are not restrained by any sense that God will judge them for their actions. However, David knows better. In a profound statement of faith in God, David declares that his enemies will be judged for their actions (vv. 7–8).

There is beautiful symmetry in God's judgment. David's enemies slandered him and used their words like arrows in order to bring about his destruction (vv. 3–4). But the reality is that God "will shoot them with his arrows; they will suddenly be struck down. He will turn their own tongues against them and bring them to ruin" (vv. 7–8). Like a boomerang, the attacks of the enemy will bounce off David and rebound upon themselves. God's justice will lead people to both proclaim the glory of God and ponder what He has accomplished (v. 9).

Go Deeper

Even though in this life the wicked may seem to get away with evil, what are you assured from this psalm? How does that help you face today's difficult and often unjust situations?

Pray with Us

Lord God, we join in David's words of praise. We echo his hope in Your justice and Your love. You are the same God who works in our lives today, giving us a hope and a future. May You forever be praised! Amen.

BOOK 2

PSALM 65

Praise God

Blessed are those you choose and bring near to live in your courts!
We are filled with the good things of your house, of your holy temple.
PSALM 65:4

Have you ever been in the situation where you know you have wronged someone and are anxious for an opportunity to apologize and ask for forgiveness? When you do finally get a chance to say you are sorry, and even restore the relationship, it comes with a huge sense of relief.

David had this experience with God. In today's reading, David praises God because "you forgave our transgressions" (v. 3). In the Old Testament, sins could be forgiven through repentance and participation in animal sacrifice at the temple. Ultimately, Jesus' death would fulfill the requirement for sacrifice. Because of His death, we too are forgiven. We have all the more reason to declare, "Blessed are those you choose and bring near to live in your courts!" (v. 4).

In verses 5–8 of this psalm, David praises God for His mighty works in creation. God formed the mountains and is able to calm the mighty power of the seas (vv. 6–7). In the ancient world, the sea was viewed as a primeval source of chaos and destruction. Even the gods were afraid of its power. But not the God of Israel. He created the sea and can easily tame it. Creation itself joyfully proclaims God's glory from morning to night (v. 8).

In the final stanza, David praises God for His bountiful provision of food and water. In the industrialized world, we are often far removed from our sources of food and don't think that much about them. But when David looked at the fertile hills and streams, he recognized God's goodness and care (vv. 9–13). God is the One who clothes the valleys with grain and the fields with flocks (vv. 12–13).

Go Deeper

What can we learn from David's words about forgiveness? How does being forgiven naturally turn into praise? Spend time in confession before God today.

Pray with Us

God, You are the Creator and sustainer of life. We pray with the psalmist who says, "God our Savior, the hope of all the ends of the earth and of the farthest seas." (Ps 65:5). May Your name be praised forever! Amen.

BOOK 2

PSALM 66

Come and See!

Praise our God, all peoples, let the sound of his praise be heard.
PSALM 66:8

Do you know your family's history? A friend of mine often recounts the story of how and why his family came to Chicago. They were a part of the Great Migration of African Americans from the South in the early twentieth century. This helps him share in the sufferings and joys of his family and community.

In today's reading, the psalmist celebrates what God has done for Israel by recounting their history. He encourages all people to "come and see what God has done!" (v. 5). He tells of God's mighty acts during Israel's exodus from Egypt and entry into the promised land (v. 6). God is to be praised because He rescued Israel and provided for them.

However, God's care involved more than just miraculous acts. God also disciplined Israel when necessary (vv. 9–11). This was also reason to praise God, as it demonstrated His love. In verse 13, the psalmist shifts from speaking about the community as a whole to what God had done in his own life. "Come and hear, all you who fear God; let me tell you what he has done for me," he declares (v. 16). He testifies that God delivered him when he was in trouble (v. 14). It's important to note that he set his personal testimony in the context of the big story of God's salvation in the Old Testament. God did not deliver him for his own sake, but so that he could participate in God's mission to the world. Part of that mission is declaring God's goodness to all people and calling them to worship.

Go Deeper
You probably enjoy telling stories of your family's history. But how often do you tell your family's God stories? Take time today to share one thing you saw God do in your family.

Pray with Us
Lord, Jesus, thank You for Your faithfulness to all generations! Thank You that Your miraculous power works from parents to children to grandchildren. We will tell of Your wonderful deeds to those who come after us! Amen.

BOOK 2

> PSALM 67

Praying for Blessing

May God be gracious to us and bless us and make his face shine on us.

PSALM 67:1

Have you ever felt like your prayer was one long wish list? "Help Aunt Katie to heal from her hip surgery. Help my daughter do well in math this year. Help. Help. Help." Are these kinds of prayers selfish? Today's reading will encourage you that bringing your requests to God is not selfish when done from the right perspective.

The psalmist begins by asking for God's blessing (v. 1). God's blessing can be best understood by reading Deuteronomy 28:1–6. In that passage, Moses describes the blessings of obedience to the covenant as resulting in children, abundant crops, large herds, and full pantries. Notice that this is not a prayer for a lavish lifestyle or excess. Rather it is a prayer that there will be plenty of food, healthy relationships, and the peace to enjoy them. We too can pray with the psalmist, "May God be gracious to us and bless us" (Ps. 67:1).

Beginning in verse 2, with the word "so," the psalmist expresses *why* God should bless us. "So that your ways may be known on earth, your salvation among all nations" (v. 2). The psalmist's desire is not merely for his own well-being or for Israel, but for the nations around Israel to know God and praise Him (vv. 3–5). God's promise to Abraham would benefit all people (Gen. 12:3). By witnessing

God's hand of blessing on Israel, others would be drawn to God. True peace and justice would only be possible when all people come under the rule of God (v. 4). The hope of this psalm will be fulfilled in Jesus. In His death, he "purchased for God persons from every tribe and language and people and nation" (Rev. 5:9).

Go Deeper
Is bringing your requests before God selfish? Why or why not? How can we go beyond the "I need" portion of our prayers?

Pray with Us
Dear God, how important it is to ask for Your blessing. So today we come before You humbly asking for Your blessing on each area of our life. We bring before You our home, our loved ones, our work, and our community. Bless us, Lord! Amen.

BOOK 2

PSALM 68

Names of God

Our God is a God who saves.

PSALM 68:20

Most of us have a number of different roles, or titles, by which we are known. I have been called a husband, father, son, uncle, professor, and a hapless Detroit Lions fan. Each of those titles gives a little understanding about part of my life. Today's reading gives insight into who God is by describing His unique characteristics. A majestic and powerful hymn, Psalm 68 begins by celebrating God's power. The psalmist describes God's care for Israel in the wilderness (vv. 7–10), His defeat of Israel's enemies (vv. 12, 18), and His residence on Mount Zion (vv. 15–18).

There are many titles used to describe God in this psalm. He is described as the one "who rides on the clouds" (v. 4). This was a title Canaanites used for their storm god, Baal. Here David uses the title for Israel's God. It's his way of saying that the Lord is the true God, not Baal. The Lord is described as "a father to the fatherless and a defender of widows" (v. 5). It is important to recognize that God uses His power to help and protect the most vulnerable in society. For many today who do not have a father figure or parent in their life, this verse is a precious reminder of God's care.

God is also called "the One of Sinai" (v. 8). God revealed Himself to Israel through the giving of the Law. Our God is one who communicates with His people. The Lord is "our Savior, who daily bears our burdens" (v. 19) and a "God who saves" (v. 20). This is most vividly seen and fulfilled in Christ's death, resurrection, and ascension. All these names are reasons to sing praise to the Lord (v. 32)!

Go Deeper

What does Psalm 68 teach us about God's transcendent power and His fatherly care for each person? What do those two qualities mean to you?

Pray with Us

How wonderful it is that You are a good, good Father! No matter what our earthly experience has been, You alone fulfill our deepest needs as a truly loving parent. You are "a father to the fatherless" (v. 5). Praise Your holy name! Amen.

BOOK 2

> PSALM 69

Save Me, God

Save me, O God, for the waters have come up to my neck.

PSALM 69:1

In Buffalo, New York, a young woman drove her car into a flooded viaduct not realizing the depth of the water. As water rushed into her vehicle, she escaped out of the window and climbed onto the roof. News cameras captured the dramatic scene as emergency crews used a rescue boat to reach the stranded woman, safely rescuing her from atop the submerging vehicle.

Sometimes life feels like that news story. When things go wrong or people attack us, we may feel like we are sinking under the pressure. David gets right to the point in his lament. He describes himself as being engulfed by deep waters, his throat is hoarse from crying out to God, and his eyes are tired from looking for God's answer (vv. 1–3). There are many reasons why he was suffering. He was threatened by enemies (v. 4), slandered and disgraced (vv. 4, 7), and scorned even by his family (v. 8).

In the depth of his suffering, David lashes out and prays that his enemies will be paid back for what they had done (vv. 22–28). This may sound harsh to our modern ears. But, as one commentator said, "We live in a culture that seeks to deny pain and death. The Psalms . . . saw that the way to hope is through fear; the way to real joy is through depression; the way to loving one's enemies is through hostility. Not around these realities but through them."[31] God does not want us to pretend like everything is okay when it is not. This psalm models a way to give our anger and desire for vengeance over to Him.

Go Deeper

Do you feel up to your neck with difficult situations? If so, this psalm provides language we can use to talk to God. The psalmist also describes the suffering of Jesus. It's because of His victory over sin and death that we can have hope, even in dark times.

Pray with Us

Today's psalm reminds us of how You suffered, Lord Jesus. While we walk through suffering in this world, it pales in comparison to the hardship You endured on our behalf. We are forever in Your debt, Lord. Amen.

BOOK 2

PSALM 70

Saving Help

May those who long for your saving help always say, "The LORD is great!"
PSALM 70:4

Sometimes we have a hard time asking for help. On more than one occasion this has caused me to get into a difficulty that I could have easily avoided. One reason why many of us struggle with asking for help is that we like to be thought of as self-sufficient.

In today's reading, David recognized that he could not solve his problems by himself. He needed God's help, and he needed it quickly! Notice the urgency in his language. He begins this short lament with the word "hasten" and ends it with the command "do not delay"! In between these two pleas he twice urges God to "come quickly" (vv. 1, 5).

David illustrates his plight by describing two groups of people. There are those who want to take his life, shame him, and discredit him (vv. 2–3). David prays that these people will be stopped in their tracks. Then there are people who rejoice in the Lord. These people never tire of declaring that "the LORD is great!" (v. 4). David prays that they will be supported and blessed. He places himself in this latter group and declares, "But as for me, I am poor and needy; come quickly to me, O God" (v. 5).

This prayer teaches us that we should recognize and confess our need for God. We are not self-sufficient and there is no shame in begging God for help. It also teaches us that in the midst of a difficult situation, we can still proclaim that "the Lord is great!" (v. 4). When we do so we are joining with the faithful throughout the ages who have testified to its truth.

Go Deeper

Compare and contrast this psalm with the story in Mark 9 where a father asked Jesus to heal his son. How can the father's reply, "I do believe; help me overcome my unbelief" (v. 24), become our own prayer?

Pray with Us

Lord, show us how to recognize our need for Your help. Help us always to turn to You in our time of difficulty. Today's psalm teaches us how to do this in a humble and honest way. Amen.

BOOK 2

> PSALM 71

I Will Praise You

> *Do not cast me away when I am old; do not forsake me when my strength is gone.*
>
> PSALM 71:9

Western society often idolizes youth and marginalizes the elderly. People spend billions of dollars on anti-aging products. This reflects a widespread anxiety about growing older. We fear the loss of significant work, the deterioration of our health, and the ability to be heard and valued.

While we do not know who wrote Psalm 71, it was someone advanced in years (vv. 9, 18). He fears being disrespected and shamed by others (vv. 1, 4, 10–11). He recognizes the loss of physical strength (v. 9) and feels vulnerable and dependent upon others (vv. 4, 11, 18). Yet this is someone who has walked with God. "For you have been my hope, Sovereign LORD, my confidence since my youth" (v. 5). In the midst of lamenting his situation, the psalmist models ways to process these fears and anxieties.

First, he looks back over his life and recognizes that God has been faithful in the past and can be trusted with the future (vv. 6, 14, 15, 17). Long experience has taught him of God's faithfulness. He can take comfort in God's continued care.

Second, he knows he has an important purpose in life. He has a responsibility to relay what God has done to the next generation. He asks God not to forsake him "till I declare your power to the next generation, your mighty acts to all who are to come" (v. 18). He can testify to God's might and power in a unique way given the perspective long years of walking with God have given him. Indeed, by the end of the psalm he has worked through his lament and turned instead to joyful praise (vv. 22–24).

Go Deeper

What can younger people learn from the experience and wisdom of older saints? If you are an older saint, how can you pass down your wisdom to the next generation?

Pray with Us

Thank You God that followers of Jesus at any age can serve Him and bless others. We come before You, young and old, with an eagerness to be used for Your glory and honor. We surrender our life to Your will. Amen.

BOOK 2

PSALM 72

Your Kingdom Come

May all kings bow down to him and all nations serve him.
PSALM 72:11

Has there ever been a perfect king or president? While history books record the achievements and the failures of those in positions of power, I'm sure we'll agree that it's difficult to find any leader who is completely without fault. In today's psalm the prayers of those seeking justice are answered with the gift of an ideal king. This prayer provides us with a vision of what such an ideal king's reign would look like.

Here the psalmist prays that the king will reflect the character of God in administering justice (v. 1). The success of this king will not be measured by his wealth, but by how he treats the poor and the needy (vv. 2, 4). This king will rescue the vulnerable from the hand of oppressors (vv. 12–14). This king's reign will be marked by prosperity for all, a long reign, and an enduring peace (vv. 3–7). His rule will extend from "sea to sea and from the River to the ends of the earth" (v. 8). Under his just and righteous rule, there will not be hunger or violence.

In Genesis 12:1–3, God promised Abram that through his offspring all the families of the earth would be blessed. That promise is fulfilled in the reign of this king. The psalmist declares, "Then all the nations will be blessed through him, and they will call him blessed" (v. 17). His praise turns to God "who alone does marvelous deeds" (v. 18). In case you haven't figured it out already, this psalm finds its fulfillment in Jesus. He is the King who will bring true peace and justice. He alone will rule over the nations (Rev. 21:25–26).

Go Deeper

Today, make a list of leaders who need your prayer. They can be leaders in your church, your community, your workplace, and in our nation. We know that God is the King of kings, and all true power and justice come through Him alone.

Pray with Us

Lord God, when we consider earthly rulers we are so often disappointed. No human authority can live up to Your perfect example. May we place our trust in You, Lord. We also pray for those You placed in authority over us. May You guide and direct their steps. Amen.

BOOK 3
PSALMS 73–89

BOOK 3

PSALM 73

A Vision of God

Blessed are the pure in heart, for they will see God.
MATTHEW 5:8

It is commonly observed that things are not always what they seem; the first appearance can be deceiving. When the author of Psalm 73 looked around him, his first impression was of a world where the wicked flourish while the godly suffer. He found himself envious of the arrogant (v. 3). It looked to him like the wicked could plot evil, engage in violence, mock God—and not only get away with it, but even thrive (vv. 4–12)!

The psalmist then examined his own life. He had labored to keep his heart pure before God (v. 13). Yet, all his labor seemed to be in vain. He experienced only affliction and pain (v. 14). Didn't justice demand that the godly prosper and the wicked be punished? Didn't Scripture teach that truth (see Ps. 1)? This led him to a crisis of faith. He worried about defaming God before others and was deeply troubled in spirit (vv. 15–16).

The turning point came in verse 17: "till I entered the sanctuary of God; then I understood their final destiny." His first impression of the world had been deceptive. The reality was that the wicked were on "slippery ground" (v. 18). Their current prosperity only masked the reality that they were under God's judgment (vv. 18–19). The psalmist also realized he was not as forsaken as he had thought. God was with him and that was a better gift than any amount of wealth (vv. 23–24). Even if his material prosperity and physical health gave way, God was still his most precious possession (v. 26). This change in perspective came from an encounter with God in worship at the sanctuary (v. 17).

Go Deeper

What sorts of emotions and circumstances distract us from spending time with God? How does a regular time of worship help us see the world properly?

Pray with Us

Heavenly Father, let us not be so weighed down by worry that we cannot see Your goodness. Thank You that You are with us. Help us understand that Your presence is the most precious thing we could ask for. Amen.

BOOK 3

> PSALM 74

Rise Up, O God!

Your wound is as deep as the sea. Who can heal you?
LAMENTATIONS 2:13

How do we engage with God when we are deeply wounded? According to the National Institute of Health, trauma can affect our "beliefs about the future via loss of hope."[32] Israel had been through a major trauma. Their cities had been plundered, portions of their population had been exiled, and the temple had been destroyed.

In response, the psalmist begins with a series of questions: "O God, why have you rejected us forever" (v. 1)? He reminds God that He had redeemed them from slavery (v. 2). God their Shepherd would protect and provide (v. 1). The psalmist takes God on a tour of the temple. He describes how the enemies had come in like lumberjacks, hacked down pillars, then burned and defiled the sanctuary (vv. 4–8). Isn't the temple where God dwelled? Was it right for God to move into a house and have it burned down? The issue for the psalmist was not so much that God had judged Israel. Rather, his anxiety was that the judgment would be everlasting.

Adding to the torment was the fact that God was silent. He had ceased to speak through His prophets (v. 9). No one knew how long this would last. At this point, the psalmist steps back and reminds himself that "God is my King from long ago; he brings salvation to the earth" (v. 12). He knew that God is capable of redeeming Israel. He draws on imagery from creation and the exodus to celebrate God's power (vv. 13–17). If God can crush the heads of Leviathan, surely He could meet Israel's needs. The psalm ends with seven imperatives begging God to remember His people (vv. 18–23). There was no answer yet.

Go Deeper

Are you currently in a position of waiting for God? What does this psalm teach you about times of waiting?

Pray with Us

Lord, we often feel Asaph's desperation in our own lives. When we are tempted to despair, remind us of Asaph's prayer—just as You did not abandon Israel, You will not abandon us. Amen.

BOOK 3

PSALM 75

The Cup of God's Wrath

"When the earth and all its people quake, it is I who hold its pillars firm."
PSALM 75:3

When I was camping in a pop-up trailer with my family, a thunderstorm came up suddenly in the night. The wind shook the canvas and rocked the trailer. We wondered how long our shelter would hold up. Thankfully, neither my family nor the trailer sustained any real damage. At times, this world can feel fragile and out of control. We might wonder if the next political or health crisis might be the end. In today's reading, the psalmist praises God because he knows that the world is in His powerful hands. In verse 3, God declares, "When the earth and all its people quake, it is I who hold its pillars firm."

One of the things that can make the world seem unstable is when arrogant and wicked people are in positions of power. In this psalm, God confronts them directly (vv. 4–5). He describes their judgment with two memorable images. He proclaims, "I will cut off the horns of all the wicked" (v. 10). The horn was a symbol of status and power. To cut off someone's horn is saying that their position and ability to influence will be removed. In contrast, God says, "the horns of the righteous will be lifted up" (v. 10).

The second image is a cup. "In the hand of the Lord is a cup full of foaming wine mixed with spices; he pours it out, and all the wicked of the earth drink it down to its very dregs" (v. 8). God's justice will one day be measured out. The New Testament teaches that Jesus is the one who drank the cup of God's wrath (Matt. 26:42). But for those who do not have faith in Christ, judgment will come (Rev. 20:11–15).

Go Deeper

What sorts of things threaten your feelings of stability? What two images does the psalmist use to remind us that God is in control?

Pray with Us

We pray the words of the hymn "A Mighty Fortress Is Our God": "And though this world, with devils filled, should threaten to undo us / We will not fear, for God hath willed His truth to triumph through us." You are in control, Almighty God; we trust You. Amen.

BOOK 3

PSALM 76

The Power of God

He breaks the spirits of rulers; he is feared by the kings of the earth.
PSALM 76:12

Investment advisers often say, "Past performance is no guarantee of future result." The phrase serves as a kind of disclaimer. Just because a particular company has performed well in the past, there is no guarantee it will do so in the future. While it may not be a sound way to make financial investments, it is a good way to judge someone's character. It is why we ask for references on job applications, or ask about the applicant's work history.

In today's reading, the psalmist applies this logic to his relationship with God. He celebrates God as awesome and powerful. God has taken up His residence in Jerusalem and from there He has defended it by breaking "shields and the swords, the weapons of war" (v. 3). We do not know what specific victory is being celebrated, but the point is powerfully made. At God's rebuke, "both horse and chariot lie still" (v. 6). The horse and chariot were the most feared weapons of the ancient world. It would be like saying, "At God's rebuke, aircraft carriers and nuclear warheads are powerless."

God's power is endless. The psalmist asks in awestruck wonder, "Who can stand before you when you are angry?" (v. 7). God's ability to defeat His enemies in the past serves as the basis of hope for the future. This psalm looks forward to the day when people from all nations will pay homage to God (v. 11). This theme comes to its fulfillment in the book of Revelation where rebellious powers and nations are decisively defeated (Rev. 19:11–21). The New Jerusalem descends from heaven, and "God's dwelling place is now among the people, and he will dwell with them" (Rev 21:3).

Go Deeper
How does God's past performance give us security? Reflect not just on what God has done for you in the past, but what He has done for His people as recorded in Scripture.

Pray with Us
We rejoice in the security of knowing that You are with us now and forever! We extol You, our all-powerful God. Your wisdom knows no bounds and Your mercy is everlasting. Amen.

BOOK 3

PSALM 77

Our Waymaker

You are the God who performs miracles.

PSALM 77:14

What do we do when the way forward looks helpless and confusing? How do we take the next step? Who will lead us? Again and again in Scripture, we see that God provides a way. It took ten terrible plagues, but Pharaoh finally decided to let Israel go free. But shortly after making this decision, Pharaoh pursued them with the might of the Egyptian army. In the meantime, God had led Israel in a rather unusual direction. Instead of taking them directly to the promised land, they went south to the Red Sea (Ex. 14:2). There they found themselves stuck with the sea in front and the Egyptian army behind. There was nowhere to turn.

In this seemingly hopeless situation, God demonstrated His power dramatically. He held the Egyptians back and parted the sea so Israel could continue their journey (Ex. 14–15). God made a way where there was no way. The memory of this mighty act of God is what brought the author of Psalm 77 out of despair. The psalmist was in a distress; he could not sleep, and his thoughts troubled him (vv. 1–6). He understood that Israel deserved God's judgment, but worried that it might be forever (v. 7). He wondered if God would forget to be merciful and compassionate to His wayward people (vv. 8–9).

To rouse himself out of this dark place, the psalmist resolved to "remember the deeds of the LORD" (vv. 11–12). Specifically, he remembered how God had led Israel in the exodus: "your path led through the sea, your way through the mighty waters, though your footprints were not seen" (v. 19). God did not take Israel down the easy path but down one that looked impossible, to demonstrate His power.

Go Deeper

When you are facing a difficult decision, where do you turn for help? How does the psalmist reinforce our need to turn to God in every situation?

Pray with Us

We praise You for Your mighty deeds! You are the Waymaker, the Miracle Worker, the God who saves. We worship You for Your mighty acts and extol You for the power You have displayed in our lives! Amen.

BOOK 3

PSALM 78

Knowing God

We will tell the next generation the praiseworthy deeds of the LORD.
PSALM 78:4

In his classic work *Knowing God*, J. I. Packer points out the difference between knowing about God and knowing God.[33] He understood that it was possible for someone to have sound theology, know the Bible well, be involved in ministry, and yet not really have a relationship with God.

One way we can know God's character is by reflecting on how He has related to His people. The psalmist in today's reading recounts God's history with His people so that the next generation would "put their trust in God and would not forget his deeds" (vv. 6–7). The goal is not just to learn history, but to trust in the God revealed by it. The psalmist reflects on God's deliverance of Israel from Egypt. He reminds them how God defeated the Egyptian army and provided for His people in the wilderness (vv. 12–16). Instead of being grateful, Israel rebelled and complained (vv. 17–19). In His grace, God continued to provide for their needs and judged them for their sins (vv. 20–31). These acts were both designed to cause repentance. Yet, Israel continued to rebel. They grieved God again and again. In response to their ungratefulness and disloyalty, God showed Himself to be slow to anger, merciful, and forgiving (v. 38).

The psalmist reflects on the time period of the judges and early chapters of Samuel. He recounts God's continued faithfulness and Israel's obstinacy. God raised up David as king to serve as a faithful shepherd (vv. 65–72). On this side of history, we know David's line also failed to be obedient, which led to exile. Yet, God promised that a Davidic king would reign on the throne of Israel forever (2 Sam. 7:11–16).

Go Deeper

What is one way you can share what you know about God with the next generation (vv. 4–8)? Consider a practical way you can pass on these important truths.

Pray with Us

God in heaven, we want to be intentional in passing on the stories of Your faithfulness to the next generation. Help us recognize opportunities to teach young people what a great God You are through the power of narrative. Amen.

BOOK 3

PSALM 79

Where Is God?

Help us, God our Savior, for the glory of your name.
PSALM 79:9

When a natural disaster like a tornado or hurricane strikes, government officials tour the areas hit hardest. One of the reasons for this is to show that they recognize the situation and intend to do something about it. Another reason is to highlight the devastation in order to arouse people's compassion so they will give to and participate in relief efforts.

In today's reading, the psalmist takes God on a tour of their devastation. This was not a natural disaster, but a resounding military defeat. The psalmist reminds God, "They have left the dead bodies of your servants as food for the birds. . . . They have poured out blood like water all around Jerusalem, and there is no one to bury the dead" (vv. 2–3). The psalmist appeals to God's compassion so He will bring relief.

At the same time, the psalmist recognizes that their defeat and the destruction of the temple were well deserved. He recognizes the "sins of past generations" and prays that God will forgive them (vv. 8–9). The psalmist longs for God's deliverance not just for his own sake, but for God's sake. The foreign powers who dominated Israel viewed their victory as a sign that Israel's God was weak and powerless. The psalmist pleads, "Why should the nations say, 'Where is their God?'" (v. 10). He looks to God as a good shepherd and prays that He will intervene to protect them. When that deliverance comes, "then we your people, the sheep of your pasture, will praise you forever" (v. 13). The Jewish people have continued to pray this psalm on the ninth of Av, which commemorates the destruction of the temple.

Go Deeper

What is lament? What emotions and needs does this type of prayer express to God? Why is it important to bring these things before His throne?

Pray with Us

"Help us, God our Savior, for the glory of your name; deliver us and forgive our sins for your name's sake. Why should the nations say, 'Where is their God?'" (Ps. 79:9–10). Amen.

BOOK 3

PSALM 80

Revive Us, O God!

Revive us, and we will call on your name.

PSALM 80:18

In the parable of the prodigal son, the wayward son recognizes his sin and comes to his senses, saying, "Father, I have sinned against heaven and against you. I am no longer worthy to be called your son; make me like one of your hired servants" (Luke 15:18–19). It is an impassioned speech, given from a place of desperation.

Psalm 80 is a kind of prodigal son psalm. The nation of Israel cries out to God in the aftermath of a crisis. While they do not directly confess sin, they recognize that their plight is due to God's judgment. They remind God, "You have fed them with the bread of tears; you have made them drink tears by the bowlful" (v. 5).

The psalmist describes the nation of Israel as a vineyard that God has carefully planted and tended (vv. 8–11). But now God has broken down its walls: "Boars from the forest ravage it, and insects from the fields feed on it" (v. 13). What God has built, He has now destroyed. The people lament, "Your vine is cut down, it is burned with fire; at your rebuke your people perish" (v. 16).

The psalmist begs God to remember that He is the "Shepherd of Israel" (v. 1). Three times he asks God: "Restore us, God Almighty; make your face shine on us, that we may be saved" (vv. 3, 7, 19).

The people know that their only hope is that God would bring about repentance and restoration. They pray, "Revive us, and we will call on your name" (v. 18). While this prayer is rooted in Israel's covenant relationship with God, we too can echo this cry.

Go Deeper

What is the story of the prodigal son? How does it connect to this psalm? What meaning does this hold for you today?

Pray with Us

We lift our faces to You even in the shame of moral failure, spiritual forgetfulness, or open disobedience. "Revive us, and we will call on your name" (Ps. 80:18). Amen.

BOOK 3

PSALM 81

True Worship

Now this is eternal life: that they know you, the only true God, and Jesus Christ, whom you have sent.

JOHN 17:3

"What have you done for me lately?" It's easy to forget how well someone has served us in the past when we are disappointed with them in the present. Some companies take this approach with their employees: "It does not matter how great of a job you did last year, or last week—what value are you bringing to the company now?" The question for us today is: How often do we take that approach with God?

Psalm 81 opens with a summons for Israel to praise God at the Feast of Tabernacles (vv. 1–4). This was a time when Israel commemorated God's deliverance in the exodus and His provision in the wilderness (v. 5). We expect the psalm to continue in celebration. But it does not. Beginning in verse 6, we get God's perspective. God reminds Israel that He freed them from slavery in response to their pleas for help (vv. 6–7). Yet, Israel did not listen to Him or follow His commands (vv. 8, 11). Instead, they worshiped other gods, followed their own counsel, and refused to give gratitude to the Lord (vv. 9, 11). You can sense God's frustration: "If my people would only listen to me, if Israel would only follow my ways" (v. 13).

In the previous few psalms, Israel often appealed to God's deliverance in Egypt as proof that God would intervene to save them again (see Pss. 77:10–20; 80:8–11). But here, God responds by reminding Israel that when He delivered them, they quickly forgot. They had a "what have you done for me lately" relationship with God. They only wanted results, while God desired a relationship.

Go Deeper
Do you have a "what have you done for me lately" relationship with God? Today, reflect on all that God has given you and spend time thanking Him.

Pray with Us
God our Savior, forgive us for our forgetfulness. Before we ask You for the things we need, remind us that You are not only a giver of blessings but also our Father and our friend. Amen.

BOOK 3

PSALM 82

God of Justice

"Rescue the weak and the needy; deliver them from the hand of the wicked."
PSALM 82:4

When thirty-three-year-old Bob Pierce was in China holding evangelistic meetings, he was introduced to an abandoned Chinese girl. After she became a Christian, the girl's father beat her and threw her out into the street. She had lost everything. Moved by her story, Bob gave the young girl the last five dollars in his pocket, promising to send more. This simple act of generosity in 1947 led to the founding of World Vision, an organization through which God's people have supported and protected millions of needy children![34] God had a plan, not just for that girl, but for Bob as well.

Psalm 82 provides a unique, prophetic look into the spiritual realm. The first verse portrays God as handing out judgment against the "gods." These are angelic beings who had been given some degree of influence in the world (Deut. 32:8–9). God judges them for showing "partiality to the wicked" and failing to "uphold the cause of the poor and oppressed" (vv. 2–3). Their failure to stand up for and protect the most vulnerable in society led to God's condemnation: "I said, 'You are "gods"; you are sons of the Most High.' But you will die like mere mortals" (vv. 6–7). This judgment is described in

Isaiah: "In that day the LORD will punish the powers of the heavens above and the kings on the earth below" (Isa. 24:21).

This psalm clearly demonstrates God's sovereignty and authority over every power and principality, whether in heaven or on earth. It also demonstrates God's heart for the weak and needy. The church today should also be concerned with care for the poor and oppressed. When we claim to have faith without works—it is no kind of faith at all (James 2:5–6,14–17).

Go Deeper

What are you doing to extend God's love to the weak and needy? Consider joining an effort in your own community to offer tangible help to those in need. Or give financial support to a worthy organization.

Pray with Us

Merciful Lord, fill us with compassion for the needy and defenseless. Show us ways to serve the weak and the poor. We seek to obey and honor You! Amen.

BOOK 3

PSALM 83

Grace in Judgment

This is good, and pleases God our Savior, who wants all people to be saved and to come to a knowledge of the truth.

1 TIMOTHY 2:3-4

The apostle Paul was under attack. He had been arrested on the false charge that he had brought a Gentile into the temple in Jerusalem (Acts 21:27–29). A group of Jewish leaders had had enough of Paul. They made a pact that they would not eat or drink until they had killed him (Acts 23:21). Paul's nephew heard about the plot and warned Paul, who was able to convince his Roman jailers to get him to safety. Because of this deliverance, Paul was able to continue his ministry in prison writing the books of 1 and 2 Timothy and Titus.

In today's reading, the nation of Israel found itself in a similar situation. A group of ten nations had formed an alliance against Israel (Ps. 83:5). The word "alliance" is the term normally translated as "covenant." These nations covenanted that they would destroy Israel "so that Israel's name is remembered no more" (v. 4). But God had also made a covenant with Israel that they would be a blessing to all the nations (Gen. 12:1–3) and that Abraham's descendants would be as numerous as the stars in the sky and the sand on the seashore (Gen. 15:5; 22:17). Would the covenant of the nations undo God's covenant with Israel?

The psalmist prays fervently that God would intervene and bring deliverance. He asks God not to be silent or aloof (v. 1). He reminds God that these enemies are God's enemies, trying to undo God's promises to Israel (Ps. 83:2–3). He asks God to defeat them just as He had in the past (vv. 9–12). God had bigger plans for these nations than simply their destruction. He prays that the nations would seek after God and come to know Him (vv. 16, 18).

Go Deeper

Are there situations you are facing that require God's intervention or deliverance? Spend some time in prayer today, bringing those situations before God and then trusting Him for the outcome.

Pray with Us

It is natural for us to crave vengeance against those who wrong us. God of justice, teach us to love our enemies so that, like Asaph, we are driven to intercede even for those who oppose us. Amen.

BOOK 3

PSALM 84

Longing for God

How lovely is your dwelling place, LORD Almighty!
PSALM 84:1

When we were engaged, my wife and I had a long-distance relationship. We lived about four hours apart by car and every weekend one of us would make the pilgrimage to see the other. All year, we would wait impatiently for the end of each week so we could be in each other's presence.

Today's reading describes the longing of the psalmist to be in God's presence in the temple: "My soul yearns, even faints, for the courts of the LORD; my heart and my flesh cry out for the living God" (v. 2). The psalmist looks with envy upon the birds who nest in the temple who get to be in God's presence continually (v. 3)! The blessed life would be in the temple, ever praising the Lord (v. 4).

The next best thing would be to make the pilgrimage to worship the Lord during the festivals (v. 5). Here, the physical pilgrimage takes on spiritual dimensions as the worshiper passes through the "Valley of Baka" (v. 6). "Baka" literally means "weeping." The worshiper travels through the valley of weeping to appear in joy and strength before God in Zion (vv. 6–7).

The psalmist feels most at home with God. "Better is one day in your courts than a thousand elsewhere" (v. 10). He would rather be a doorkeeper in the temple than in a position of power with the wicked (v. 10). He recognizes that his relationship to God is the most vital part of life. God is his protector and provider (v. 11). The one who is truly blessed is one who puts their trust in the Lord alone (v. 12).

Go Deeper

What role does the local church play in your relationship with God? Although we can worship God on our own, Paul reminds us that on this side of the cross the church corporately is the "dwelling in which God lives by his Spirit" (Eph. 2:19–22). Are you longing to join in worship this week?

Pray with Us

Lord Almighty, thank You for giving us Your church, where we can worship and serve You. We admire the psalmist's hunger for Your presence and ask for the same fervency in our own hearts. Amen.

BOOK 3

PSALM 85

Justice and Forgiveness

Show us your unfailing love, LORD, and grant us your salvation.
PSALM 85:7

Have you ever needed to ask someone for forgiveness? It is a difficult place to be in because it means admitting that you have done something wrong. You also might not know how the offended person might react. You might ask for forgiveness, but will they grant it?

In Psalm 85, Israel found itself in the position of having to once again ask God for forgiveness and restoration. They begin by reminding God of how He has forgiven them in the past (vv. 1–3). There are many examples to choose from: the golden calf incident, the period of the judges, or the capture of the ark. Israel knew that God is a forgiving God, but they also knew that He is just and would allow the consequence of sin to run its course.

Here Israel begs, "Restore us again, God our Savior, and put away your displeasure toward us" (v. 4). They asked God to turn from His just anger and to demonstrate His love toward them (vv. 5–7). In verse 8, God responds, "I will listen to what God the LORD says; he promises peace to his people, his faithful servants—but let them not turn to folly." God not only promises to restore His people but also to give them a vision of His desired future.

Of course, it is possible to have peace without justice, truth without love, or justice without compassion. God, however, presents a future where "love and faithfulness meet together; righteousness and peace kiss each other" (v. 10). In other words, this future will be a time of true well-being. God's love, faithfulness, righteousness, and peace will come together in an embrace that permeates the entire world.

Go Deeper

Do you sometimes underestimate your own sinfulness and even overestimate the sinfulness of others? Why is it difficult for us to see our own mistakes? How does focusing on God's character help change that?

Pray with Us

Father God, may we never live a day without thanking You for sending Your Son to take our place on Calvary. Because of Christ's sacrifice, we experience love, faithfulness, righteousness, and peace every day. Amen.

BOOK 3

PSALM 86

An Anchor for the Soul

When I am in distress, I call to you, because you answer me.

PSALM 86:7

Have you ever felt that in the grand scheme of what God is doing in the world, your problems seem almost too small for God to care about? We sometimes assume that God must be more concerned with what the rulers of the world are up to or the plight of those who are suffering far more than we are.

In Psalm 86, the psalmist knows that God has a plan for the world. Halfway through the psalm we read, "Among the gods there is none like you, Lord; no deeds can compare with yours. All the nations you have made will come and worship before you, Lord" (vv. 8–9). The psalmist affirms the truth that the Lord is unique. There is no other god like Him! He also looks forward to the day when all nations, not just Israel, will bow before the Lord in worship and adoration.

The psalmist asks the Lord to help him understand and apply these precious truths to his life (vv. 11–12). Yet in the midst of these lofty theological reflections, the psalmist also asks that the Lord would be active and involved in his own life and with the issues he was facing. He was being attacked either physically or verbally by malicious enemies (v. 14). He humbly asks God to, "Hear me . . .

and answer me . . . guard my life . . . have mercy on me" (vv. 1–3). He knows that God is big enough to care about both the big issues of the world and the future as well as his own daily struggles.

Indeed, our daily struggles can help point us to God. The trouble the psalmist was in caused him to reflect on God's compassionate and gracious nature (v. 15). That is why we can be confident to turn to Him in any situation. He has invited us to do so. The sovereign ruler of the universe is also our source of help and comfort (v. 17).

Go Deeper

God is big enough to care for all the pressing issues in the world today, *and* He cares about your personal struggles! Rest in that incredible truth, and entrust your worries to God.

Pray with Us

Today, with the psalmist, we pray, "Among the gods there is none like you, Lord; no deeds can compare with yours. All the nations you have made will come and worship before you, Lord" (86:8–9). Amen.

BOOK 3

> PSALM 87

The God of Zion and the God of the Nations

In the last days the mountain of the LORD's *temple will be established as the highest of the mountains; it will be exalted above the hills, and all nations will stream to it.*

ISAIAH 2:2

Have you ever had a worship song at church stop you in your tracks? At a church I visited recently, we sang "Grace Wins" by Matthew West. In the chorus, several biblical characters are named—the prodigal son, the thief on the cross, and the woman at the well. It then proclaims that "grace wins" in each of their situations. I found myself wondering, *Is that really true? What about Judas? What about Goliath?* The song provoked me to think more deeply about what the grace of God actually is and how it functions in the midst of a fallen world.

Psalm 87 would also likely have stunned worshipers in ancient Israel. It opens conventionally enough by proclaiming the Lord's love of Zion (v. 2). This would be reassuring to Israel. God has a special affection for His people and their land. But as it continues, the message expands. God Himself speaks in this psalm and proclaims that Rahab (a nickname for Egypt), Babylon, Philistia,

Tyre, and Cush would be given as status as God's people. "The LORD will write in the register of the peoples: 'This one was born in Zion'" (v. 6).

These nations were Israel's enemies. They often oppressed and exploited the people. Egypt had enslaved Israel, Babylon had exiled them, and the Philistines were Israel's perpetual enemies. Yet from the beginning God had called Abraham so that through him, "all peoples on earth will be blessed" (Gen. 12:3). Israel was reminded in their worship that God has a plan for the nations, even their enemies. One day, people from every nation will stream to Zion to worship the Lord (Isa. 2).

As followers of Jesus, we also are called to love our enemies and pray for those who persecute us (Matt. 5:43–47). We can do that because that is how God acts toward His enemies as well, causing the sun to rise and the rain to fall on the just and the unjust (Matt. 5:45). One day, God will redeem people from every people, nation, and language (Rev. 5:9).

Go Deeper

How should God's heart for the nations impact your life today? We can be grateful that because of the work of Jesus, our citizenship is in heaven (Phil. 3:20).

Pray with Us

As the hymn says, "O to grace how great a debtor daily I'm constrained to be."[35] God, Your grace is beyond comprehension. Thank You for the grace You have given to us. We did not deserve it, and we are eternally grateful. Amen.

BOOK 3

> PSALM 88

Darkness Is My Closest Friend

The light shines in the darkness, and the darkness has not overcome it.
JOHN 1:5

After the death of his wife, C. S. Lewis processed his grief by journaling about his sadness and anger toward God and the world. He later felt his journal might help others who were grieving and published it under a pseudonym with the title *A Grief Observed*. Generations of readers have found consolation in Lewis's raw and honest portrayal of his life with God even in the midst of deep loss.

The life of faith will often include periods of intense pain and loneliness. In today's reading, the psalmist expresses the deepest and darkest lament in the Psalter. He gives voice to the grief that even some of the most faithful of God's servants endure. As commentator Marvin Tate expressed, "Long trails of suffering and loss traverse the landscape of human existence, even for the devoted people of God. There are cold, wintry nights of the soul, when bleakness fills every horizon and darkness seems nearly complete."[36]

The psalmist is overwhelmed by troubles and seems fixated on death: "I am set apart with the dead, like the slain who lie in the grave, whom you remember no more, who are cut off from your care" (v. 5). Even worse, he believes that God is the one who has put him in this situation (vv. 6–7). He called upon the Lord day after day, but heard no response (vv. 9, 14). God seems far away and hidden. Not only is he cut off from God, but he is also estranged from other people. He ends his lament with the line, "darkness is my closest friend" (v. 18).

Go Deeper

How does the psalmist describe his deep grief? What can we learn from this psalm about walking through dark times in our own lives?

Pray with Us

Lord of Peace, we know You can raise the dead, but in dark affliction we sometimes doubt that You can face our probing questions. Give us courage to talk to You about the things we fear to contemplate. Amen.

BOOK 3

PSALM 89

Remember God's Promises

I will sing of the LORD's great love forever.

PSALM 89:1

Much of our life of faith is spent living in between God's promise and its future fulfillment. All through the Bible, God makes big promises and then asks His people to live in faith. God promised Abraham he would be the father of a great nation when he had not even had a child yet and was already seventy-five years old (Gen. 12:1–4). It would be over twenty years before this promise was fulfilled.

In today's reading, Ethan the Ezrahite begins with a resounding word of praise. For the first thirty-seven verses, Ethan recounts the steadfast love of the Lord. He praises God for creation, His justice and righteousness, and for choosing David as Israel's king (vv. 1–20). God had anointed David and gave him victory over his enemies (vv. 20–23). The poet celebrates God's covenant with David whom he had appointed "to be my firstborn, the most exalted of the kings of the earth" (v. 27). God had even promised that if David's descendants were unfaithful, God would punish, but never abandon them (vv. 30–37).

The psalm takes an abrupt shift in verse 38. After celebrating God's promises to David, he wonders where God is now: "But you have rejected, you have spurned, you have been very angry with your anointed one" (v. 38). Reflecting the crisis of the Babylonian exile, Ethan describes how Israel has been defeated. From his perspective, it seemed like God had renounced the covenant He made to David (v. 39). We know (of course) that in the New Testament a future descendant of David would fulfill all of these promises and so much more (Luke 1:32; Acts 13:22–23).

Go Deeper
Are you worried about your future? Notice that even though God's promises to David seemed broken, the psalmist did not reject God. Instead, he turned to God in prayer (Ps. 89:46–51).

Pray with Us
You have assured us that we will suffer in this life, yet calamity still takes us by surprise. Father, hold us close when we doubt Your presence, and fortify our faith when we question Your kindness. Amen.

BOOK 4
PSALMS 90–106

BOOK 4

PSALM 90

Life and Death

A thousand years in your sight are like a day that has just gone by,
or like a watch in the night.

PSALM 90:4

From the fountain of youth to the philosopher's stone, humans have long been obsessed with finding a way to cheat death and achieve immortality. For most people, the solution to the problem of death is to just not think about it, to live as if life will never end.

In today's reading, Moses provides us with wisdom to live well. This wisdom comes from reflecting on the contrast between humanity and God. Moses reflects on the eternality of God. God is literally older than the hills (v. 2). Indeed, He is their Creator. While a thousand years is enough time for about forty generations of humans to live and die, for God it is merely "like a watch in the night" (v. 4).

Human life is fleeting. It is like grass in a desert climate that springs up in the morning but withers and dies under the afternoon sun (v. 6). Moses reminds us, "Our days may come to seventy years, or eighty, if our strength endures; yet the best of them are but trouble and sorrow, for they quickly pass, and we fly away" (v. 10). This mortality is a result of sin going back to Genesis 3. Because of our sin, we are all under God's wrath (vv. 7–9).

Often people and human institutions act as if they will endure forever. Wisdom means embracing mortality and recognizing that true life can only be provided by God. Moses asks God to "satisfy us with your unfailing love" (v. 14). He understands that we are dependent upon God for any lasting significance to our life or work (v. 17).

Go Deeper
This psalm is honest! It reminds us that life is short, hard, and ends in death. How did the gospel change this forever? Read Jesus' promise in John 10:28.

Pray with Us
No reality is too harsh while You are on the throne, God. "Make us glad for as many days as you have afflicted us, for as many years as we have seen trouble" (v. 15). We have counted the cost, and You are worth it all. Amen.

BOOK 4

PSALM 91

Safely Home

Whoever dwells in the shelter of the Most High will rest in the shadow of the Almighty.

PSALM 91:1

Every day we are reminded that human life is incredibly fragile. As we look at the world, there are endless threats pressing near—disease, war, famine, and spiritual forces of evil, to name a few. It can be easy to focus on these potential dangers and retreat in fear.

In the Psalms, we see a realistic description of these threats, but also a strong reminder of God's loving care and protection. Psalm 91 is a profound call to trust in God, even in the midst of danger. The psalmist declares that the safest place in the world is to dwell "in the shelter of the Most High" and to "rest in the shadow of the Almighty" (v. 1). Because of this, we do not need to fear "the terror of the night, nor the arrow that flies by day" (v. 5). These real dangers are not beyond God's supervision.

Some of the most profound statements about God's protection are found in this psalm (worth bookmarking in your Bible!). The psalmist declares that "no harm will overtake you, no disaster will come near you" (v. 10). Our daily experience may seem to indicate otherwise. Indeed, many of the godliest people in the Bible experienced persecution and suffering. So, how are we to understand this language? Perhaps it is best understood referring to God's ultimate defeat of evil at the return of Christ. Writing from a prison cell and close to death, Paul uses similar language: "The Lord will rescue me from every evil attack and will bring me safely to his heavenly kingdom" (2 Tim. 4:18).

Go Deeper

It is easy to look at our circumstances and experience fear. What truths do the psalmist and Paul remind us of that will encourage us during these times?

Pray with Us

You have already made good Your promise to deliver us from evil; our future with You is secure and eternal. Even when we ask for Your protection, we understand that nothing can separate us from You. Amen.

BOOK 4

> PSALM 92

Made to Worship

You, Lord, are forever exalted.

PSALM 92:8

Music is one of the most engaging human activities. When we sing or play an instrument our whole being is engaged—our mind, our heart, and our body. Music unites us. In a choir, a group of unique individuals become one as they sing. Maybe that is the main reason God created music, because it is a wonderful way to praise Him!

Psalm 92 begins with an announcement that it is good to praise and make music to the Lord (v. 1). Today's reading encourages us to use the best of our musical skill to proclaim God's loyal love and faithfulness day and night (vv. 2–3).

God's loyal love and faithfulness are displayed in His deeds (vv. 4–5). While no specific acts of God are mentioned, the Old Testament is full of examples. God created the world, called Abraham, delivered Israel, provided food and water in the desert, and revealed the Law to Moses (just to name a few). Meditation on these gracious acts leads the psalmist to step back in awe and proclaim, "How great are your works, Lord, how profound your thoughts!" (v. 5).

There are two possible responses to this call to praise. The wicked will act foolishly and refuse to acknowledge God. They are "senseless" (v. 6). This word is normally used to describe animal behavior.

Just as animals cannot step back and perceive God at work, the fool also cannot see beyond himself. Like green grass, the wicked may seem like they are flourishing for the moment, but their destruction is sure (v. 7).

In contrast, the righteous will grow like a majestic cedar or hearty palm tree planted in the temple court (v. 12). They will flourish because they are close to God and stay connected to Him (v. 13).

Go Deeper

What is your favorite praise song or hymn? Why is it meaningful to you? Sing a song of praise to God today!

Pray with Us

O Lord, You do not need our worship, but You delight in it—and we delight to praise You! We laud Your justice and proclaim Your righteousness. May Your name be extolled in every nation, tribe, and tongue! Amen.

BOOK 4

PSALM 93

Who's in Charge?

Mightier than the thunder of the great waters, mightier than the breakers of the sea—the LORD on high is mighty.

PSALM 93:4

At a restaurant I recently visited, there was a plaque with a photo of the manager in the front entryway. Under the photo was a brief message from the manager stating his goals for the restaurant. If these goals were not met, he invited people to reach out to him. He was in a position to make things better.

In some ways, the opening of Psalm 93 is similar to the message on that plaque. It reminds us who is really in charge. The psalm proclaims, "The LORD reigns, he is robed in majesty... indeed, the world is established, firm and secure" (v. 1). Despite how things may look to us in the moment, from our limited perspective, the reality is that God is on the throne.

In the heart of the poem, the psalmist portrays the image of powerful and chaotic seas (v. 3). Imagine standing on the beach during a storm with waves pounding on the shoreline. It makes you feel pretty small. In the ancient world, the seas were symbols of chaos, evil, and destructive forces. Hostile nations are often described in the same language (e.g., Ps. 46:6). The psalm acknowledges our experience that the world often does not look like God is in control. Yet the following verse declares that God is even mightier than the "thunder of the great waters" (v. 4).

Sometimes we need to be reminded that God reigns over all, that no forces of evil or schemes of the enemy can thwart His plans for the world or for our lives. God's rule is most clearly seen in the life of Jesus. When the disciples were terrified because of a storm they experienced, Jesus rebuked them: "'You of little faith, why are you so afraid?' Then he got up rebuked the winds and the waves, and it was completely calm" (Matt. 8:26). He is indeed mightier than any storm we might experience (v. 4).

Go Deeper
What would it look like for you to trust that God is on the throne today? What worries or anxieties could you give over to Him?

Pray with Us
Lord, when the thunder booms and the lightning crashes, remind us that You are in control. No matter what may happen to us today, we do not need to fear for You are with us. You are in charge of the waves. You can save us. Amen.

BOOK 4

> PSALM 94

Judge of All

Rise up, Judge of the earth; pay back to the proud what they deserve.

PSALM 94:2

Have you ever tried to play hide-and-go-seek with a two-year-old? It can be pretty comical. I remember playing the game with my son at that age and found him standing next to his bed with his face buried in the covers. He thought, "If I cannot see my dad, he must not be able to see me!" While this is cute in a toddler, it would be foolish for an adult to hide in that way.

In Psalm 94, the wicked seem to have this perspective toward God. Because they do not see God immediately judging them for their acts of oppression and violence, they conclude that God must not have noticed. "They say, 'The LORD does not see; the God of Jacob takes no notice'" (v. 7).

However, the psalmist knows that God is the judge of all the earth. The question for him is not, "Will God judge?" But rather, "How long, LORD, will the wicked, how long will the wicked be jubilant?" (v. 3). He encourages the wicked to change their thinking. Instead of acting like fools, they should pursue wisdom (v. 8). He reminds them that God is the one who created the ear and the eye, surely He also can see and hear (v. 9)! Nothing escapes God's notice, He "knows all human plans" (v. 11).

Blessed is the one who submits to God's discipline and learns from God's Word (v. 12). This person knows that their only hope against the wicked is to trust in the Lord (vv. 16–17).

Go Deeper

Do you find yourself looking the world and asking, "How long, Lord?" Make a list of the things that make you long for God to take action. Then use that list as your prayer prompt today.

Pray with Us

God in heaven, You have claimed vengeance for Your own. May we love those who hate us enough to tell them about Your Son, that they might be forgiven for the very acts they have hurt us with. Amen.

BOOK 4

PSALM 95

Wholehearted Worship

Come, let us sing for joy to the LORD; let us shout aloud to the Rock of our salvation.

PSALM 95:1

University of Michigan football fans have nicknamed their stadium "the Big House." When the team scores, the fans fill the space with so much cheering and shouting the sound can be overwhelming. One of the reasons why people enjoy watching the college game in person is to experience being part of such an enormous crowd united in the support of their team and celebrating their victories.

In today's reading, the psalmist calls Israel to join in worship: "Come let us sing for joy to the LORD" (v. 1). The psalmist describes singing, shouting, and making music to God. This is not a time for silent meditation, or half-hearted singing. No! This is a full-throated, raucous, and joy-filled expression of devotion to the Lord.

God is to be praised with full enthusiasm because he is far above all other "gods" that people worship. The majestic mountains and powerful oceans owe their existence to God. He can hold them in the palm of His hand (vv. 3–5). God is not only the Creator of all things, He is also "our God" (v. 7). He cares for us like a shepherd cares for his flock (v. 7). The only appropriate response is to drop to our knees in humble submission (v. 6).

Our worship should be more than just words. God requires wholehearted devotion. The psalmist reminds Israel of the exodus generation, who saw God's power firsthand. This group of people quickly turned their back on God, grumbling against Him (Ex. 17:1–7). They even wished that they had never been redeemed from Egypt. Because of that, God judged them by not allowing them to enter the promised land.

Go Deeper

Do you praise God with as much energy and enthusiasm as you give your favorite sports team? What is true worship in God's eyes?

Pray with Us

Our God is an awesome God! Fill us with Your joy, Father. Stir our hearts and minds with the power of Your might; may we be too overwhelmed with You to keep silent. Amen.

BOOK 4

PSALM 96

Sing to the Lord!

Sing to the Lord, praise his name; proclaim his salvation day after day.
PSALM 96:2

Have you ever wondered why some people propose marriage at large gatherings like a professional baseball game? They might want to make the moment memorable by choosing such an unusual setting. But they might also feel it is not enough to declare their love to their beloved in private, they want the whole world to know.

Today's psalm is a rousing call to praise God. The psalmist commands "all the earth" to praise the name of God all the time (vv. 1–2). God has done wonderful things for Israel (v. 3). He has chosen to dwell in Israel's midst (vv. 6, 8). He is far superior to any other so-called god (v. 4). It was not enough for Israel to keep the truth about this God to itself. Israel needed to proclaim His name and His works to all the nations.

"Ascribe to the Lord, all you families of nations, ascribe to the Lord glory and strength" (v. 7). The nations are invited to come into the temple courts and present offerings to the God of Israel (v. 8). They are commanded to join Israel in worshiping the Lord (v. 9).

But it is not enough to just have Israel and the nations worship God, creation itself is invited to join the chorus! The psalmist calls on the heavens and earth, the seas and fields, and even the trees to proclaim the greatness of God (vv. 11–12). Our joy at the salvation God has provided overflows, inviting others to join us in giving thanks to the Lord. It is best to acknowledge God's rule now because He is coming to judge (v. 13).

Go Deeper

Describe the overall mood of this psalm. What does it teach you about how to worship God?

Pray with Us

How can we stay silent when the mountains and seas, the fields and the trees, cannot contain their praise? We raise our voices with the rest of creation to honor and worship You! Amen.

BOOK 4

> PSALM 97

God Is King

For you, LORD, are the Most High over all the earth.

PSALM 97:9

The United States is deeply divided politically. One reason is that many people look to political victories as their primary source of hope for the nation. When their party wins an election, they are elated. When their candidate of choice is defeated, they fall into despair.

Today's reading provides us with the good news that it is not a human person who will ultimately decide our future. The good news is that "the LORD reigns" (97:1)! While humans act like they are in control, Psalm 97 reminds us that God created the universe and it directs us to worship Him alone (v. 6).

We must also name and denounce the idols that compete for our loyalty and allegiance (v. 7). God will not have a rival. For Israel this meant avoiding the worship of Baal and Asherah, the gods of the culture around them. While most people in Western culture today are not tempted to bow down to a literal idol, we often live as if power, money, fame, or material possessions are the most important things in life. No one should be able to worship God with full-throated praise and cling to idols at the same time.

The kind of praise modeled for us in Psalm 97 is humbling. It puts us in our place and reminds us that we are not God. Rather, we owe our allegiance to God alone. When we embrace that truth, we can rejoice in His faithful rule in the present even as we wait for His ultimate rule to be established on the new heavens and new earth (98:9). Recognizing the fact that God reigns should lead us to rejoice (97:8). We can rejoice because we know that God is gracious and just.

Go Deeper

What idols are competing for your attention? What things do you place your hope in? Spend time today rereading this psalm and acknowledging God as the ruler of everything in your life. Rejoice that our God reigns!

Pray with Us

Lord, Your name is above any other name, and You are worthy to be praised. How can we give our loyalties to any other person or thing? You alone are worthy; make Yourself foremost in our affections. Amen.

BOOK 4

PSALM 98

Joy to the World

Shout for joy to the LORD, all the earth, burst into jubilant song with music.
PSALM 98:4

"Joy to the world the Lord is come; Let earth receive her king!" Are you singing the tune in your head now? "Joy to the World" is one of the most recognizable Christmas hymns. Yet, it was not written to celebrate Christmas. In 1719, Isaac Watts published a book of poems based on different psalms. "Joy to the World" was inspired by Psalm 98 to celebrate Christ's second coming. Over a hundred years later, the poem was set to music and became the Christmas carol we know and love today.

Psalm 98 calls Israel to "sing to the LORD a new song" (v. 1). God had accomplished a mighty act of salvation for Israel (vv. 1–2), a new song was required to celebrate it properly. Israel was to use the best of their lyrical and musical prowess to celebrate what the Lord had done. Singing with just a voice was not enough. They also needed to include string and wind instruments (vv. 5–6). The salvation was likely a military victory. Yet, the goal was not just to celebrate the defeat of other nations. Part of the purpose of the song was to let the nations know and rejoice in the Lord (v. 7).

The victory Israel had just experienced pointed forward to a greater victory when the Lord would come and bring in justice and righteousness for all people (v. 9). The world groans under the weight of sin and injustice, so the hope of the righteous rule of God when all wrongs would be made right is truly a reason for all of creation to raise their voice in jubilant praise (vv. 7–8).

The hymn writer got this message exactly right: "No more let sins and sorrows grow; Nor thorns infest the ground; He comes to make his blessings flow; Far as the curse is found!" When the Lord Jesus returns, He will redeem the world from the effects of sin. At that time, all will know "The glories of his righteousness; And wonders of his love!"

Go Deeper

Have you ever tried to write out a song of praise or thanksgiving for something God has done in your life? How do these moments point us forward to our ultimate hope?

Pray with Us

Lord, we long for Your return. At that time, You will redeem this world from the effects of sin. You will right all that is wrong. And we will bask in Your love. What a wonderful day that will be! Amen.

BOOK 4

PSALM 99

A Just and Merciful God

*Exult the LORD our God and worship at his holy mountain,
for the LORD our God is holy.*
PSALM 99:9

In 1741, George Frideric Handel was deeply in debt after a string of musical failures. When he was on the verge of going to debtor's prison, his friend Charles Jennens wrote the text of an opera based on the life of Jesus Christ and gave it to Handel to write the music. In just twenty-four days, Handel wrote the musical masterpiece *Messiah*.[37] The famous "Hallelujah" chorus celebrates the fact that God is the King of kings who will reign forever and ever.

Psalms 93–99 celebrate the Lord's kingship. You'll notice a common refrain in these poems: "The LORD reigns" (Pss. 93:1; 96:10; 97:1; 99:1). You may also recognize this section of Scripture as the "Hallelujah" chorus of the Psalter. Because God reigns over all, Psalm 99 encourages all people to "praise your great and awesome name" (v. 3). The fact that God reigns is the best possible news. He is a ruler who is just and does what is right (v. 4). He is also a King who listens to His people. The psalmist reminds us of Moses, Aaron, and Samuel who often interceded for the people of Israel (v. 6). God heard their prayers and answered them.

God also showed Himself to be forgiving. Israel sinned by

worshiping a golden calf on Mt. Sinai (Ex. 32). Despite their deep breach of faithfulness, God forgave the people and continued to reside with them (Ex. 34). God however also punishes sin (v. 8). These two truths are not contradictory. God is both just and merciful. The animal sacrifice in the Old Testament foreshadowed the greater sacrifice of our Lord Jesus in the New Testament. Sin can be both punished and forgiven because God made a way for us.

Go Deeper
What does Psalm 99 tell us is the best possible news? What do we have to celebrate?

Pray with Us
We pray with the psalmist today: "Enter his gates with thanksgiving and his courts with praise; give thanks to him and praise his name. For the LORD is good and his love endures forever" (Ps. 100:4–5). Amen.

BOOK 4

PSALM 100

Our True Identity

Worship the LORD with gladness; come before him with joyful songs.
PSALM 100:2

Disassociate amnesia is a rare condition in which people cannot remember basic information about themselves—their name, relationships, or personal history. While this condition is rare, it is more common for us to forget basic truths about our relationship with God.

Psalm 100 is a praise psalm. At the heart of this poem are some important reminders for us if we have developed any spiritual amnesia. The psalmist challenges the congregation to "know that the LORD is God" (v. 3). The word "LORD" here is the personal name, "Yahweh." We need to remember and acknowledge that there is a God. This God has a name and an identity. Yahweh is the God who created the universe, who covenanted with Abraham, who delivered Israel from Egypt, and who sent His Son to die for our sin. We do not worship a nameless, generic deity, but a God who has made Himself known.

The psalmist reminds us that, "It is he who made us, and we are his" (v. 3). Yahweh is not only the Creator of the universe, but He also fashioned each one of us (Ps. 139:13). We have an identity that is secure. We have been created by a loving God and we belong to

Him. That is a status that we cannot earn but is received by faith.

The final reminder in this verse is "we are his people, the sheep of his pasture" (v. 3). God has called us into community. God has a relationship with His people. We were never meant to live the life of faith alone—just me and God. All through Scripture, God has given His people a group identity to be a part of—Israel and the church.

These are wonderful reasons to worship the Lord. We can join with God's people all through history and confess, "For the LORD is good and his love endures forever; his faithfulness continues through all generations" (v. 5).

Go Deeper

What foundational truths about God does this psalm teach us? Have you gone through seasons when you have forgotten who God is or that you belong to Him?

Pray with Us

God, we have so many reasons to worship You. Thank You for designing us to live in community, for grafting us into Your church. Help us never to take this for granted, but to join with Your people to praise You. Amen.

BOOK 4

> PSALM 101

Holy Worship

He has shown you, O mortal, what is good. And what does the Lord require of you? To act justly and to love mercy and to walk humbly with your God.

MICAH 6:8

"Power corrupts," as the saying goes, "and absolute power corrupts absolutely." It is true that there is something about the human condition that makes power dangerous. In his commentary on the Psalms, the Reformer John Calvin observed: "Although kings are not born fools, yet they are so blinded by their dignity, that they think themselves in no respect indebted to their subjects."[38] These corrosive effects of power can even be seen not only in government but also in the church.

In today's reading, David affirms a commitment to justice and holiness. He resolves to worship God by how he lives, by leading "a blameless life" (v. 2). He commits himself to extend this commitment to his position as king. He will run his "house" or kingdom with integrity as well (v. 2). A part of running his kingdom with integrity included rooting out corrupt administrators and officials. David declares that "the perverse of heart shall be far from me; I will have nothing to do with what is evil" (v. 4).

David's examination of his house and kingdom should prompt an examination of our own. Can we say, "I will be careful to lead a blameless life" (v. 2), or that we "will not look with approval on anything that is vile" (v. 3)? David desires to surround himself with people who are honest in their communication, who have integrity in their motives, and who will serve people faithfully (vv. 6–7). For David, living with integrity was not just about being a good king, it was an act of worship (v. 1). And this choice would not be made once, but "every morning" (v. 8).

Go Deeper

Are you conducting your affairs with a blameless heart (v. 2)? Are you looking with approval on vile things (v. 3)? How should following God affect our speech, our purchases, our entertainment choices?

Pray with Us

Holy God, we ask You to cleanse our minds. Grant us fresh discernment to recognize what is vile and around us. Make our ways blameless, so that we too can say, "I will have nothing to do with what is evil." Amen.

BOOK 4

> PSALM 102

Clinging to God

Jesus Christ is the same yesterday and today and forever.
HEBREWS 13:8

A few years ago, the building of the church I grew up attending was torn down. I was saddened to think that the place where I had spent so much of my childhood, where I had encountered God, would be demolished. While I realized that it was just a building, this event evoked a longing for permanence. What, in life, does not change?

Psalm 102 has a unique title. It tells us that it is a prayer for afflicted people who need to pour out a lament to God. It is comforting to know that God provided us with models for how to relate to Him in our suffering. The psalmist here is clearly in distress. He describes the transience of his life, comparing it to smoke and withered grass (vv. 3–4). His body aches from suffering to the point where he forgets to eat (vv. 3–5). Additionally, he is cut off from any sense of community. He compares himself to a desert owl, or a bird alone on a roof (vv. 6–7). This image illustrates his sense of social isolation. He recognizes that his suffering is not his alone, but part of the suffering of God's people (vv. 12–16). This psalm was likely written during the Babylonian exile, when many in Israel felt abandoned by God.

The psalmist finds solace by reflecting on God's attributes. He reminds himself that the Lord is on the throne (v. 12). Despite how desperate his personal situation might be, God does not change, "but you remain the same and your years will never end" (v. 27). This is good news because God promises not to give up on His people. He would forgive and restore Jerusalem (vv. 21–22).

Go Deeper

Do you feel isolated or alone? Take comfort in the truth that God does not change. God cared enough for you to send His Son to die for your sins. This same God will never change and is faithful to keep His promises.

Pray with Us

Father, You loved us enough to send Your Son to suffer in our stead. Help us to be longsuffering for Your sake. Give us love for You that carries us through the grief and loneliness we must inevitably face. Amen.

BOOK 4

PSALM 103

Amazing Grace

For as high as the heavens are above the earth, so great is his love for those who fear him.

PSALM 103:11

In 1835, a music publisher named Charles Bradlee created a tune to help children learn the alphabet. Using a theme by Mozart, Bradlee copyrighted the tune that children all over the United States sing to learn their ABCs. Just like Charles Bradlee, the Israelites knew that one of the best ways to teach truth about God was through poem and song. Since most of ancient Israel was not able to read, songs were especially important.

In verses 3–5 of today's reading, David outlines many of God's gifts that Israel had experienced through the ages: forgiveness, healing, redemption, and renewal. These gifts flow from God's nature. God is "compassionate and gracious, slow to anger, abounding in love" (v. 8). The word for "love" here is difficult to capture in English. It means being devoted to someone in a covenant commitment. It is a kind of love that is for better or worse, richer or poorer, in sickness and in health.

Sometimes we may picture God as only loving and forgiving to the exclusion of other attributes He has. David does not do so here. He reminds us that God is also "slow to anger" and just

(vv. 6, 8). "Slow to anger" reminds us that anger is at times God's appropriate response rooted in His covenant love. His anger is in the context of a deep understanding of our frailty as humans. God "remembers that we are dust" (v. 14). This does not mean that we are unimportant, but rather that God is mindful of our limitations. The proper response is to join with the angels and heavenly hosts in joyful praise (vv. 20–21).

Go Deeper
Why is forgetfulness dangerous in our relationship with God? How does singing help us remember God's faithfulness?

Pray with Us
We praise You for the times You have provided, even when we lost hope. We worship You for the ways You have sustained us, even when our strength failed. We honor You for the mercies You have granted, even when we didn't want them. Amen.

BOOK 4

PSALM 104

This Is My Father's World

*How many are your works, Lord! In wisdom you made them all;
the earth is full of your creatures.*

PSALM 104:24

My family enjoys watching nature shows together. It is stunning to see the diversity of animals and habitats that exist in the world. While most science shows do not give God the credit for creation, watching them often leads my family to have conversations about how creative and powerful our God is.

The author of Psalm 104 would have made a good scientist. He carefully observes many aspects of the created world in order to praise God. He observes the water cycle. He recognizes that rain is what sustains the life of animals and makes crops grow (vv. 10–14). The water cycle is not an impersonal process, but rather is evidence of God's faithfulness and kindness.

The author notices that some animals come out and hunt in the night and sleep during the day, while people work during the day and sleep at night (vv. 19–23). Everything has its proper time and place. The ocean is still unexplored in many places. And, on occasion, the news will report of a new species that's been discovered. It is a reminder to us that God cares about the animal world. He did not simply create them for humans. Rather, this psalm reminds us that God created them for His own delight (vv. 24–26). Indeed, the psalmist proclaims, "May the LORD rejoice in his works" (v. 31).

The sheer diversity and wonder of the created world should inspire us to join with the psalmist in praise to God. Surely, "how many are your works, LORD! In wisdom you made them all; the earth is full of your creatures" (v. 24). Today's reading is a good reminder to open our eyes and allow the wonder of creation to inspire us to praise God.

Go Deeper

Take time today to observe and celebrate God's magnificent creation. While today human sin has corrupted God's creation (v. 35), we can look forward to its redemption and restoration when Christ returns (Rom. 8:22–25).

Pray with Us

God the Creator, may we rejoice in science for what it teaches us about You. May each new discovery humble us, reminding us that we are merely discovering the work of Your hands. Amen.

BOOK 4

PSALM 105

Family History

*He remembers his covenant forever, the promise he made,
for a thousand generations.*

PSALM 105:8

One of the things my family loves to do at gatherings is tell stories. We recall the quirky personalities of loved ones who have departed. We talk about how couples met and got married. We tell our children some of the funny things older members of our family did when they were young. These stories, told again and again, play an important part of forming family identity and binding us to one another. We have a shared history.

Psalm 105 recounts and celebrates God's history with Israel. It is closely connected to the psalm before it and the one after it. These three psalms follow the sequence of Israel's history from creation and the fall (Ps. 104) to God's call of Abraham to the conquest of the land (Ps. 105), ending in Israel's apostasy and exile (Ps. 106). Today's reading shares family stories of God's faithfulness.

The psalmist calls people to "remember the wonders he has done" (v. 5). He highlights the promise God made to Abraham to give his descendants the land of Canaan (vv. 8–11). This promise is seen as a primary factor in Israel's history. When there was a famine, God had sent Joseph ahead of his family to Egypt to provide for them (vv. 16–22). When Israel was enslaved, God freed them (v. 27). God led and guided them in the wilderness and brought them into the promised land (vv. 42–45). One theme runs through this psalm: God keeps His promises! When Joseph was sold as a slave, God had not abandoned him, but used him to deliver His people. When Israel was enslaved to a major superpower, Egypt, God demonstrated His glory by delivering them.

Go Deeper

Despite how desperate things may look, why should God's people never give up hope? How does looking ahead to Christ's return shape our view of the future?

Pray with Us

Today we meditate on the promises You have brought to completion. Your Word is a testament to Your honor and faithfulness. Looking back enables us to look forward with confidence, knowing that You still keep Your promises. Amen.

BOOK 4

> PSALM 106

O God, Our Help in Ages Past

Give thanks to the LORD, for he is good; his love endures forever.
PSALM 106:1

Why is it so easy for us to forget the victories and miracles of our past when faced with the troubles of today? In yesterday's reading, the psalmist narrated Israel's history with an emphasis on God's faithfulness. Today's reading continues with a different emphasis.

This psalm was likely written during the exile to Babylon which had created a crisis of faith for many in Israel. God had judged them as a nation. They asked, "How should we respond to His judgment?" The psalm begins by offering praise to the Lord (v. 1). The psalmist declares that he is going to recite God's "mighty acts" (v. 2). We are prepared for the recital of the miracles God performed for Israel. In a sense, that is exactly what the psalmist does, describing the exodus from Egypt, the crossing of the Red Sea, and the conquest of the promised land. However, this time the emphasis is not so much on the miracles, but on how Israel responded. Israel consistently fell into unbelief.

After the miracle of the Red Sea, the psalmist laments, "But they soon forgot what he had done" (v. 13). Israel failed to enter the promised land right away because "they did not believe his promise" (v. 24). After the conquest of the land, Israel worshiped idols, sacrificed their children to false gods, and "shed innocent blood" (vv. 34–39).

Despite all this, God was patient. He judged them in order to bring about their repentance. Again and again, God offered grace. But Israel's sin culminated in the exile (v. 47). The psalmist calls Israel to repent and to praise God for His faithfulness even while longing for deliverance (vv. 47–48).

Go Deeper

How did Israel respond to God's judgment? How should we respond when God acts in judgment toward us or our nation?

Pray with Us

Lord God, we hesitate to judge Israel for their unfaithfulness, because we so often fall into unbelief ourselves. We praise You that our salvation depends on Your faithfulness to us. May we grow evermore faithful to You. Amen.

BOOK 5
PSALMS 107–150

BOOK 5

> PSALM 107

Unfailing Love

Let the redeemed of the Lord tell their story.
PSALM 107:2

"Worship is natural to the Christian," said J. I. Packer, writing about the Psalms. "The habit of celebrating the greatness and graciousness of God yields an endless flow of thankfulness, joy, and zeal."[39] In the Psalms we find joy-filled expressions of praise. We also hear honest words of suffering and sorrow. The Psalms give language to the whole range of our human experience, helping us bring every emotion before God.

Psalm 107 focus on God's grace and forgiveness after decades of exile because of their sin, God restored Israel to her land. The psalm uses four images to depict the horrors of exile. Living in exile is compared to wandering in desert wastelands with no food or water (vv. 4–5). The exile is then compared to a prisoner in chains working like a slave (vv. 10–13), and all hope seemed lost. In a rather different image, the exile is compared to a fool who suffers because of their folly (vv. 17–18). Finally, exile is compared to a merchant on a ship caught in a storm (vv. 23–26).

In each situation, people cried to the Lord for help, and He delivered them. He gave food and drink to the desert wanderer (v. 9). He brought the prisoner out of darkness (v. 14). He rescued the fool (v. 20). God calmed the waves and "stilled the storm to a whisper" (v. 29).

In each case, people were delivered not because they deserved it, but because they called upon the Lord. Again and again, we are called to praise God for his "unfailing love" (vv. 8, 15, 21, 31), which comes to its fulfillment in the life, death, and resurrection of Jesus.

Go Deeper

How has God delivered you in past situations? Spend some time today reflecting on what truths you learned about God during that time. Then, praise Him for His care for you!

Pray with Us

We give thanks to You, Lord, for You are good. Your love endures forever! We are among the redeemed; move us to tell our story as the psalmist urges, so that others can know Your goodness! Amen.

BOOK 5

PSALM 108

Help Me, God!

Save us and help us with your right hand, that those you love may be delivered.

PSALM 108:6

Have you ever felt like God's promises were not being fulfilled in your life? Perhaps you think of Jesus' statement, "Peace I leave with you; my peace I give you" (John 14:27), but you do not feel any sense of peace in the moment. Or, even though Jesus said, "Surely I am with you always, to the very end of the age" (Matt. 28:20), it is difficult to sense His presence.

In Psalm 108, David took parts of two other psalms he had written to compose a new work (Pss. 57:7–11; 60:5–12). In this new song, David struggled because it looked like God had not kept His promise. God had promised Israel that the land of Canaan would belong to them (Gen. 12:7). Yet, as David surveyed the region, Moab and Edom threatened Israel and the Philistines were living in the promised land (v. 9). Where was God in this?

Despite the discouraging situation, David resolves to praise the Lord (vv. 1–5). He reminds himself that God is more loving, faithful, and exalted than he can imagine (vv. 4–5). He also reminds himself of God's promises (vv. 7–9). God had promised to give the land of Canaan to Israel as an inheritance. From this vantage point, David then pointedly articulates his bewilderment, "Is it not you, God, you who have rejected us and no longer go out with our armies?" (v. 11). David takes his doubts and frustration directly to God because he knows that ultimately God is loving, faithful, and powerful (v. 13). What David does not do is to walk away from his faith in God or quit engaging God in prayer.

Likewise, in our own walk of faith, it's normal to experience moments of doubt and confusion regarding what God is or isn't doing in our own life or in the world. In those times, we should remind ourselves of what we know to be true about God from Scripture. God has also invited us to bring those doubts and concerns openly to Him. He is big enough to handle our laments.

Go Deeper

The Bible does not deny that we will experience times of doubt and frustration. Are there any concerns in your life that you need to bring before Him?

Pray with Us

O God, sometimes we feel like David. We look at the puzzling situations in our own life or in the world around us and ask, "Where are You in all of this?" Help us in those times of doubt to remember who You are and what You have promised. Keep us faithful! Amen.

PSALM 109

Living in an Unjust World

For he stands at the right hand of the needy, to save their lives from those who would condemn them.

PSALM 109:31

When I first started praying through the Psalms, I used to get tripped up on psalms like Psalm 109. In this psalm David seems vengeful and angry. How could David pray that his enemies' children would become wandering beggars (v. 10)? There are a couple of important perspectives to keep in mind.

First, humans are sinful and often treat each other in terrible ways. A casual glance at news headlines on any given day will confirm this truth all too clearly. In Psalm 109, David had suffered at the hands of people who falsely accused him (v. 2). This was a serious situation that could potentially be life-threatening. David also informs us that he was not their only victim. These people "hounded to death the poor and the needy and the brokenhearted" (v. 16). How should we respond in this type of situation? How should we pray in the face of deep human evil directed against us?

Second, what David does in this psalm is communicate his anger, hatred, and frustration before God. He is honest about how he feels. Sometimes when we are deeply wounded disturbing thoughts and feelings well up in us. David takes those desires and lays them before God in a straightforward way (vv. 6–20). By doing this, David makes his anger against his enemies a part of his relationship with God. It is reassuring to realize that God is big enough to handle our honesty. David begs God to act in this situation and then, appropriately, leaves his circumstances in God's hands.

The New Testament clarifies that Jesus not only hears prayers like this from us, but He himself experienced injustice. Like David, Jesus was falsely accused and betrayed by someone He loved (vv. 4–5).

Go Deeper

Do you struggle with bitter feelings toward those who have wronged you? Follow David's example and bring those emotions, honestly, before God. Then pray that He will go before you in that difficult situation, showing you how to respond and acting on your behalf.

Pray with Us

God of Justice, though You have laid claim to vengeance, we still grapple with the injuries of evil directed at ourselves. We ask for Your justice upon those who harm us—and also for the power to extend love and forgiveness to them. Amen.

BOOK 5

PSALM 110

The Coming Messiah

Now there have been many of those priests, since death prevented them from continuing in office; but because Jesus lives forever, he has a permanent priesthood.

HEBREWS 7:23–24

Do you have a favorite psalm? If you took a poll of the writers of the New Testament, their favorite psalm would be this one. Psalm 110 is quoted directly eleven times and alluded to at least fourteen times in the New Testament. It was quoted so often because it helps us understand Jesus as both priest and king.

David opens the psalm with a prophetic tone: "The LORD [Yahweh] said to my lord" (v. 1). Who is David talking about? What "lord" would be greater than David himself? The answer is the future Messiah, as Jesus Himself indicated (Matt. 22:41–46). God had promised David that the throne of His kingdom would endure forever (2 Sam. 7:16). This pointed to a descendant of David that would redeem Israel, usher in a messianic kingdom, and fulfill these promises.

What would this king be like? One of the biggest surprises in this prophetic message is that the future king would also be a priest (v. 4). The combination of the offices of priest and king would have been difficult to understand in the context of the Old Testament. Priests were from the tribe of Levi while kings were from Judah. Only in the person of Jesus does this psalm become fully understandable (Heb. 7:11–17). David points to the figure of Melchizedek as a forerunner of a different kind of priesthood (v. 4; cf. Gen. 14:18–20).

The messianic King will bring in justice and rule over the nations (vv. 5–7). There is an "already and not yet" dynamic with this promise. Jesus has defeated sin and death through His resurrection (Eph. 1:19–21). Yet, we await His coming when His rule will be established over all when the "kingdom of the world has become the kingdom of our Lord and of his Messiah, and he will reign for ever and ever" (Rev. 11:15). Jesus will be the kind of leader that we have always longed for. He will rule in justice and peace providing redemption and deliverance for all who trust in Him.

Go Deeper
Why was this psalm so often referenced in the New Testament? How should the hope of Jesus' coming shape our lives today?

Pray with Us
Lord Jesus, You came to fulfill so many promises. What a privilege it is for us to live on this side of the story. We know how You came to live among us and to lay down your own life so that we could be redeemed. Hallelujah! What a Savior! Amen.

BOOK 5

> PSALM 111

The Alphabet of Praise

Great are the works of the LORD; they are pondered by all who delight in them.

PSALM 111:2

In the original Hebrew, Psalms 111 and 112 are alphabetic acrostics. Each line begins with a letter of the Hebrew alphabet from A to Z. This structure communicated the idea of completeness. The psalmist wanted to praise God from A to Z.

In Hebrew, the opening word of Psalm 111 is "Hallelujah!" The goal of this song is to remind the people of some of the reasons they have to praise the Lord. Praise can begin in contemplation upon what God has done (v. 2). God's mighty works are recorded in Scripture for our benefit. We can remember how He delivered Israel from Egypt. We can reflect on how He provided manna and quail for them to eat in the desert (v. 5). God's works demonstrate that He is "gracious and compassionate" (v. 4).

God can be praised because of His faithfulness. He provided Israel with the land of Canaan (v. 6). He has been faithful to the covenant promises He has made (v. 5). He also revealed His word to Israel (v. 7). God can be known through creation, through His acts in history, and through His word. God's word is "trustworthy" and "established for ever and ever" (vv. 7–8).

The right response to all that God has done is committing ourselves to Him. The psalmist reminds us that "the fear of the LORD is the beginning of wisdom" (v. 10). The word *fear* here does not mean terror or fright. Rather it refers to trusting in the Lord and obeying His commands. We should have a sense of awe, reverence, and wonder toward God. Some kinds of fear motivate us to run and hide. However, the fear of the Lord should motivate us to draw closer to God, to lean into His presence. Most importantly, it should lead us to submit our lives to His Word. As we do so, we grow in wisdom and understanding (v. 10). The more deeply we know God, the more reasons we have to continue to praise (v. 10).

Go Deeper

Try your hand at praising God from A to Z. This can be a fun game to play with children as well. Name one thing that begins with each letter for which you can thank God.

Pray with Us

Thank You for preserving the beauty of nature, even after the fall. Thank You for granting us direct access to You. Thank You for the friends and family You have given us. Thank You for the eternal paradise You have promised us. Amen.

BOOK 5

> PSALM 112

A Portrait of Faith

Praise the LORD. Blessed are those who fear the LORD, who find great delight in his commands.

PSALM 112:1

Often, we learn best by example. Psalm 111 ended by declaring that the "fear of the LORD is the beginning of wisdom" (v. 10). But what does it look like to fear the Lord in practice? Psalm 112 provides us with a cameo or a snapshot of someone who has decided to live in fear of the Lord.

The person who fears the Lord is blessed and flourishes in their lives. This flourishing is described as having children who are "mighty in the land" and "wealth and riches" in their houses (vv. 1–2). At times, God may bless His faithful children in this way. A life of wisdom often has practical real-world benefits. This psalm also recognizes that this is not always the case in this life. The ultimate fulfillment of God's promise will only be realized at Christ's return.

The person who fears the Lord lives a life characterized by generosity and care for the poor (vv. 5, 9). This care for the poor goes hand in hand with a commitment to justice (v. 5). Their character and values are modeled after God's. They are "gracious and compassionate" to others (v. 4).

A person who fears the Lord may encounter trials and suffering in life. But in those moments, they know that they are not alone, for "Even in darkness light dawns for the upright" (v. 4). Most surprisingly, fear of the Lord enables you to face the rest of your life without fear. Many live in fear of what could happen—a lost job, an unexpected sickness, or a financial crisis. The faithful are not immune to these aspects of living in a fallen world. But those who fear the Lord "will have no fear of bad news; their hearts are steadfast, trusting in the LORD" (v. 7). Their circumstances may change, but they know that the faithfulness of the Lord remains the same. They trust that one day, the Lord will visit His people and bring in justice and peace (v. 10).

Go Deeper

Have you ever seen a believer face bad news with confidence and trust in the Lord? What did that look like?

Pray with Us

Lord God, thank You for Your promise of a hope and a future in You. When life does not turn out the way we desire, we listen to Your Word. Even when we experience bad news, we have "no fear" because our "hearts are steadfast, trusting in the LORD" (v. 7). Amen.

BOOK 5

> PSALM 113

Who Is Like the Lord?

> *From the rising of the sun to the place where it sets,*
> *the name of the Lord is to be praised.*
>
> PSALM 113:3

Psalm 113 opens with a rousing call to praise. The psalmist declares that God's praise should be broadcast "from the rising of the sun to the place where it sets" (v. 3). This is a stunning claim. Should the Lord be praised in Philistia? Yes, even in Philistia. Should the Lord be praised in Egypt? Yes, in Egypt. Should the Lord be praised in Iowa? Brazil? Bangladesh? Yes, from the east to the west!

The Lord is worthy of worship from all people because there is no one like Him (v. 5). One of things that makes God so unique is that even though He is more powerful and exulted than anyone in the universe, "he raises the poor from the dust and lifts the needy from the ash heap" (v. 7). He cares deeply about people that we are often quick to ignore. The powerless and broken are especially noticed by Him.

Psalm 113 begins a series of psalms that are traditionally used at Passover to celebrate Israel's exodus from Egypt. It is likely that Jesus and His disciples sang Psalms 113–118 as a part of the Last Supper (Matt. 26:30). God heard the cries of His people and delivered them. He humbled Pharaoh and made the needy rejoice.

This theme comes to its fulfillment in the gospel. The apostle Paul said, "Not many of you were wise by human standards; not many were influential; not many were of noble birth. But God chose the foolish things of the world to shame the wise; God choose the weak things of the world to shame the strong" (1 Cor. 1:26–27). If God notices the weak and vulnerable, that is a perspective that we should have as well. Praise God today for His provision and care!

Go Deeper

Today's psalm provides another fun activity you can practice by yourself or with children. Take a roam around the house or the neighborhood, asking in each location if God should be praised. "Should God be praised in the kitchen?" "Should God be praised in the den?" Yes!

Pray with Us

Wherever we are—the verdant Appalachians, the great Midwestern plains, the majestic Sierra Nevada—nature praises You, the Creator. We lift our voices with the hills, proclaiming Your greatness. Amen.

BOOK 5

PSALM 114

We Remember

Tremble, earth, at the presence of the Lord,
at the presence of the God of Jacob.
PSALM 114:7

At a specific point in a traditional Passover meal, the youngest child will ask, "Why is this night different from all other nights?" This question allows the rest of the people at the meal to respond by telling the story of how God rescued Israel from Egypt. God's people did not sneak out of Egypt under cover of darkness but marched out boldly from their oppressors trusting in what God had done. It is vital to tell and retell what God has done to one another so that we do not forget.

Psalm 114 is the second psalm in this series traditionally used to celebrate Passover (Ps. 113–118). In the space of a few brief verses, it recounts the story of the exodus, wilderness wanderings, and conquest of the land (vv. 1–4). God not only defeated the Egyptians, but He also parted the Red Sea, stopped the waters of the Jordan, and brought forth water from a rock (vv. 3–4, 8).

In verses 4–5, the psalmist pauses to ask, "Why was it, sea, that you fled? Why, Jordan, did you turn back? Why, mountains, did you leap like rams, you hills, like lambs?" This childlike question reinforces an important point. The mountains and sea did not flee in awe of the might of Israel. Israel did not save themselves. Instead, it was the presence of the Lord (v. 7). The Lord gets the glory and the credit for the salvation that Israel experienced. Just like the earth is called to tremble before the Lord, we are to stand in awe of Him as well.

The Lord Jesus was the perfect Passover Lamb (John 1:29). Through His death and resurrection, He has redeemed us from slavery to sin (Rom. 6:3–10). Today we can join with the heavenly chorus and celebrate His achievements, "Worthy is the Lamb, who was slain, to receive power and wealth and wisdom and strength and honor and glory and praise!" (Rev. 5:12).

Go Deeper

Even if you do not celebrate Passover, you can participate in this retelling of God's goodness and protection. What are some ways God has worked in your life or the life of your family?

Pray with Us

Lord, just as You have been our help in days gone by, we know You will be with us in the days to come. Thank You for loving us with Your careful eye on each step we take. Help us to rest in that knowledge so we can trust You with our future. Amen.

BOOK 5

PSALM 115

Trust in the Lord!

Not to us, Lord, not to us but to your name be the glory.
PSALM 115:1

Most people do not like working for an employer who micromanages them. This may be in part because we don't like to be told what to do. But another reason is that micromanagement communicates a lack of trust. Because these managers do not trust their employees, they want to control them.

Today's reading vividly describes an idol. These images of gods were everywhere in the ancient world. The reason people created idols was because they wanted to have some control over the gods. If they could be assured of the god's presence in idol form, they could make offerings to it, move it where they wanted it to go, and generally exert some control over it.

But there's a problem! When you make a god that you can control, the god can only do what the human created it to do. It is limited by its maker. These "gods" look like they have eyes, ears, noses, mouths, hands, and feet but they cannot use them (vv. 4–7). The tragic outcome of the worship of these gods is that the worshipers become like the idols that they have made—spiritually dead (v. 8).

The psalm opens with the words, "Not to us, Lord, not to us but to your name be the glory" (v. 1). This is a reminder that worshiping

God begins in humility. Three times this psalm calls Israel to "trust in the LORD" (vv. 9–11). The Lord is the living God who can act. He remembers and will bless His people (vv. 12–13). Israel did not create the Lord; rather He created the heavens and the earth (v. 15).

Go Deeper

Are you ever tempted to believe that you can control God? How can you exhibit your trust in God in your prayers? God desires to bless His people. With the psalmist, let's "extol the LORD, both now and forevermore" (v. 18).

Pray with Us

"It is not the dead who praise the LORD, those who go down to the place of silence; it is we who extol the LORD, both now and forevermore" (Ps. 115:17–18). Lord, You brought us from death to life. We extol Your name! Amen.

BOOK 5

PSALM 116

Can I Get a Witness?

I love the LORD, *for he heard my voice; he heard my cry for mercy.*

PSALM 116:1

When I was a child, our church held services on Sunday evening. The service had a unique element in it. Often, the pastor would ask if anyone would like to share how God had been at work in their life. Listening to respected adults share about God in such a personal way made a huge impact on me. They would tell of answered prayers or how God had comforted them during a troubled time.

Psalm 116 is a testimony. We do not know exactly what kind of trouble the psalmist was facing, but he describes his desperate situation with great emotion: "The cords of death entangled me, the anguish of the grave came over me; I was overcome by distress and sorrow" (v. 3). Death seemed like a real possibility.

But when the psalmist cried out to God for help, God answered. God was true to His character. The psalmist rehearses the attributes of God from Exodus 34:6–7 (v. 5). In contrast to God's faithfulness, people are often untrustworthy (v. 11). But God hears prayer and responds. God's deliverance prompted the psalmist to publicly proclaim what He had done (vv. 13–14).

In this context, verse 15 stands out as a bit odd. It says, "Precious in the sight of the LORD is the death of his faithful servants." You might say to yourself, "Didn't he just pray for deliverance from death?" The word *precious* here is better understood as "costly." That is, the Lord understands the cost to the community of faith when a believer dies. This is one of the reasons God spared him in this situation.

Go Deeper

Has God always answered your prayers in the way you wanted? When that happens, this psalm is a good reminder that God's ways are higher than our own. Consider how can you tell people know what the Lord has done so their faith can be encouraged.

Pray with Us

Today, we remember the way Your plans have proven to be a blessing to us, even when we thought we needed something else. Remind us not to keep these things to ourselves, but to proclaim Your goodness to our fellow believers. Amen.

BOOK 5

> PSALM 117

Let the Nations Rejoice!

Praise the LORD, all you nations; extol him, all you peoples.
PSALM 117:1

On November 19, 1863, Abraham Lincoln delivered a speech as part of the dedication ceremony of Soldiers' National Cemetery at Gettysburg. His speech was only two minutes long and comprised 271 words. Even though it was brief, the President's speech had a huge impact. It is often quoted, alluded to, and has become an important part of our American heritage.

Psalm 117 might be the shortest chapter of the Bible, yet it also has a profound meaning out of proportion to its length. The psalm opens with a call to praise. Notice that it is not directed at Israel or the worshiping community. Instead, the psalmist calls the nations to praise Yahweh, the God of Israel (v. 1)! This psalm reminds Israel that God's desire was always to reach the nations through Israel. God called Israel not because He rejected the nations, but so that the nations could eventually join Israel in true worship (Gen. 12:3). The apostle Paul picked up on this teaching. "Christ has become a servant of the Jews on behalf of God's truth, so that the promises made to the patriarchs might be confirmed and, moreover, that the Gentiles might glorify God for his mercy" (Rom. 15:8–9).

The psalmist does not just call the nations to worship God but gives them some reasons to do so as well: "For great is his love toward us" (v. 2). The word *great* is a strong one and better translated as "prevailed." God's love has prevailed in a fallen world. His commitment to provide salvation for all people is unshakable (v. 2).

This psalm gives us a helpful way to think about evangelism. In sharing the gospel, we are calling people to come and join us in the worship of the true God. This is what we were created for. Praise God that in His mercy, He has made a way for us to be reconciled to Him.

Go Deeper

Who are some people in your life that you could share the gospel with? Imagine what it would be like to have them join you in worship!

Pray with Us

We are told, Lord God, that one day every knee will bow before You. On that day, there will be people from every tribe and every nation. What a wonderful day that will be! We pray for our friends and family members who do not know You. Open their eyes, Lord, so they can join us for eternity. Amen.

BOOK 5

PSALM 118

He Is God!

Give thanks to the LORD, for he is good; his love endures forever.
PSALM 118:1

Easter Sunday is the most joyful celebration in the Christian calendar. On that day believers remind one another that we live in a world where Jesus has risen from the dead. His resurrection demonstrates that God has defeated our greatest enemies: sin, Satan, and death.

Psalm 118 is the final song in the series traditionally used to celebrate Passover (Pss. 113–118). In this song of thanksgiving, the worship leader calls all Israel to confess that God's faithful love endures forever (vv. 1–5). Israel was not delivered from Egyptian slavery because they had a more powerful army or because they had a more brilliant military tactics. Instead, it was because of their trust in the Lord. The psalm reminds Israel that "it is better to trust in the LORD than to trust in humans. It is better to take refuge in the LORD than to trust in princes" (vv. 8–9).

As Israel streamed toward the temple to celebrate Passover, they remembered not only God's deliverance from Egypt, but of His work in saving them from many foes in their history: the Philistines, Midianites, and the Amalekites to name just a few (vv. 10–14). Remembering what God has done in the past helps Israel to trust

Him with their present and future.

As the psalm celebrates what God has done in the past, it also looks forward to a future deliverer (vv. 22–26). When Jesus was faced with the unbelief and opposition of the teachers of the law and priests, He reminded of them of this psalm, "Haven't you read this passage of Scripture: 'The stone that the builders rejected has become the cornerstone; the Lord has done this and it is marvelous in our eyes'?" (Mark 12:10–11). God's salvation demands a response of faith and gratitude.

Pause today and thank God for what He has done in the past and what He has promised to do in the future. "Give thanks to the LORD, for he is good; his love endures forever" (v. 29).

Go Deeper

What words start and end Psalm 118? "Give thanks to the LORD, for he is good; his love endures forever" (vv. 1, 29). How does this inspire you to pray today?

Pray with Us

God, You show us the meaning of faithfulness. You have promised to redeem us from our sins, to give us new life, and to return to take us home. We give thanks for the already fulfilled promises that assure us You will fulfill others. Amen.

BOOK 5

> PSALM 119:1-88

Precious Words

I rejoice in following your statues as one rejoices in great riches.
PSALM 119:14

Imagine that you spent your entire life studying Scripture and trying to live it faithfully. What would your life look like? How would it change the way you relate to God and others? Psalm 119 shows us what it looks like to love the Lord and His Word.

Psalm 119 mentions God's Word 176 times: "I remember, LORD, your ancient laws, and I find comfort in them" (v. 52). The psalmist uses eight different words to refer to Scripture: law, statutes, ordinances, commands, words, decrees, promises, and judgments. The psalmist also refers to himself 176 times. But there is one more important repetition. The word *You* is used to reference God 232 times. The psalmist is celebrating His relationship with God through the gift of His Word. "Teach me knowledge and good judgment, for I trust your commands" (v. 66).

Psalm 119 is the longest chapter in the Bible, and it is carefully constructed. Each stanza starts with a different letter of the Hebrew alphabet. So, the first eight lines all start with the equivalent of the letter "A." The next with the letter "B" and so on. This is a celebration of God's Word from A to Z!

As the psalmist immersed himself in Scripture, he discovered that God's Word is righteous (vv. 7, 62, 75), faithful (v. 30), good (v. 39), trustworthy (v. 66), true (v. 69), and precious (v. 72). Because of this, he values Scripture above all things. "The law from your mouth is more precious to me than thousands of pieces of silver and gold" (v. 72). Certainly, the gift of God's Word is something to treasure!

Go Deeper
Do you consider your Bible the most valuable thing you own? Give thanks to God today for the gift of His written Word. Tomorrow we will examine the impact that a lifetime of meditation on Scripture had on the psalmist.

Pray with Us
"Direct me in the path of your commands, for there I find delight. Turn my heart toward your statutes and not toward selfish gain. Turn my eyes away from worthless things; preserve my life according to your word" (Ps. 119:35–37). Amen.

BOOK 5

> PSALM 119:89-176

Words of Life

How sweet are your words to my taste, sweeter than honey to my mouth!

PSALM 119:103

Relationships change us. If we have a close friend or spouse that we share life with, it is inevitable that they will impact how we think and behave. In Psalm 119, the author has had a close relationship with God through studying His Word. He has immersed himself in Scripture and now crafts a poem testifying the enormous impact Scripture has had on him. How has he been changed?

The psalmist recognizes his deep dependence on God for all things, even asking God to help him understand His Word. He declares, "I am your servant; give me discernment that I may understand your statutes" (v. 125). As he grew in his knowledge of God's Word, his dependence on God for understanding grew as well (v. 105).

The psalmist delighted in and loved Scripture. Ten times he uses the word "delight" in reference to God's Word. He regularly confesses that he loves Scripture: "Oh how I love your law! I meditate on it all day long" (v. 97). Or, "Their hearts are callous and unfeeling, but I delight in your law" (v. 70). The wicked here are described as unfeeling, while the psalmist is filled with delight. Apart from God, people tend to love the wrong things. One of the benefits of meditating on God's Word is that we grow to love what God loves and hate what He hates.

The author expresses a wholehearted devotion to Scripture. This means that he does not just crack it open once in a while, but it is his persistent meditation. He reflects on it at night (v. 55), midnight (v. 62), all day long (v. 97), and even seven times a day (v. 164)!

Go Deeper

How do you act when you are devoted to someone? That is the kind of devotion the psalmist expresses here. May we also grow in our love for God's Word and allow it to change us!

Pray with Us

We are awed by the psalmist's devotion to Your Word, Lord. We ask for the same passion and intimate knowledge of Scripture. Teach us to meditate on Your Word day and night, internalizing the truths of Scripture. Amen.

BOOK 5

PSALM 120

Longing for Peace

In fact, everyone who wants to live a godly life in Christ Jesus will be persecuted.

2 TIMOTHY 3:12

Imagine being an ancient Israelite about to embark on a journey to Jerusalem for one of the pilgrimage feasts. Travel was slow, difficult, and fraught with danger. Yet, there was also the hope and joy of arriving at the temple to worship the Lord with the congregation. Psalms 120–134 all share the title "A Song of Ascents." These fifteen psalms were intended to be used as pilgrimage songs as one ascended to Jerusalem. This journey was both physical and spiritual.

The journey starts in a bleak place. Psalm 120 is a harsh poem. The psalmist looks upon the world and sees that it is full of liars (v. 2). Lies are terribly destructive. When we are surrounded by lies, we may even start to believe them. The psalmist pleads with God, "Save me, Lord, from lying lips" (v. 2). He laments, "Woe to me that I dwell in Meshek, that I live among the tents of Kedar" (v. 5). Both of these places were far from Israel (Ezek. 27:13; Jer. 2:10). In this hostile place, the psalmist longed for peace but those around him desired only violence (vv. 6–7). The first step back toward faith is to turn away from the lies of the world.

Often, we too may feel that the world is not our home. Like

creation itself, we can also groan under the weight of sin (Rom. 8:22). The psalmist turns from the lies of those around him and turns to God (v. 2). One word for this is "repentance." The psalmist has turned from the sin and evil around him and turned toward God, our only source of hope and salvation. He reminds himself that one day, God will make all things right. Justice will be done (vv. 3–4). He does not need to be afraid or to fall into despair. This psalm expresses the longing that we all have to be at our true home in the presence of the Lord Jesus (2 Cor. 5:1–10).

Go Deeper

If you ever feel broken over the suffering and evil in the world, you are not alone. Psalms like this give us words to express our grief and can help us turn our hearts to the Lord.

Pray with Us

God, we come to you in deep grief for the sinful condition of our world. Like the psalmist, we are surrounded by lies. We realize that this condition is evident in our own heart as well. How often we fail You. We come to You in repentance for ourselves. Keep us faithful, O God. Amen.

BOOK 5

PSALM 121

Looking for Help

I lift up my eyes to the mountains—where does my help come from?

PSALM 121:1

When my youngest daughter was two, she cut her cheek and needed stitches. As the doctor started to administer the medical care she needed, she eyed at her mother and me with a pleading look. She wanted us to get her out of this rather strange and uncomfortable situation. When we are scared or in distress, we naturally look for someone who can help us.

In Psalm 120, the poet is in a difficult situation. He is being attacked by "lying lips" and "deceitful tongues" (v. 2). Words are powerful. They can create hope and express joy. They can also cut and wound, creating strife and conflict. That is the scene here. While the psalmist desires peace, his enemies lie to provoke war (v. 7). Lies and deception are difficult to combat. It is easy to feel helpless when we face opposition. What can be done?

Psalm 121 serves as a kind of response to the plight described in Psalm 120. The psalmist declares, "I lift up my eyes to the mountains—where does my help come from? My help comes from the Lord, the Maker of heaven and earth" (vv. 1–2). Psalms 120 and 121 are part of the "Psalms of Ascent" (Pss. 120–134). This group of psalms was written for pilgrims making their way to one of the annual festivals at the temple in Jerusalem. So, when the psalmist says that he lifts his eyes to the mountains, he is thinking of Jerusalem. He is looking to the Lord. The psalm ends with a promise of protection. God cares deeply for His people, and He will protect them (vv. 5–8).

Go Deeper
Are you facing a tough situation? If so, the psalmist's advice is powerful: "Lift up your eyes!" How does looking "up" to God who created the universe give us confidence to face our current situation?

Pray with Us
"My eyes fail, looking for your promise; I say, 'When will you comfort me?' Though I am like a wineskin in the smoke, I do not forget your decrees. How long must your servant wait?" (Ps. 119:82–84). Help us as we wait to trust in You. Amen.

BOOK 5

PSALM 122

City of Peace

I rejoiced with those who said to me, "Let us go to the house of the Lord."
PSALM 122:1

For thousands of years Jews and Christians have made pilgrimages to Jerusalem. It is easy to understand why. Jerusalem plays a central role in both the Old and New Testaments. It is the place where Abraham was called to sacrifice Isaac, where David brought the ark of the covenant, where the temple was built, where Jesus was crucified, and where Pentecost took place. In the Old Testament it was the place where God chose to dwell (Deut. 12:4–5; Ps. 135:21).

Three times a year, Israelites were to make a pilgrimage to Jerusalem to worship at the temple. These times were a high point in their lives. "I rejoiced with those who said to me, 'Let us go to the house of the Lord'" (v. 1). To become close to the presence of the Lord was a privilege and a joy. Part of the reason for Israel's joy was the unity brought by worshiping together. David describes Jerusalem as a city "closely compacted together" (v. 3). That might sound like urban congestion to us, but it was a positive image for him. God's people were united in Jerusalem to "praise the name of the Lord" in obedience to His Word (v. 4).

The psalm ends with a prayer for peace. This is a play on the name *Jerusalem*, which means "city of peace." *Peace* in Hebrew means more than just the absence of conflict. It is a rich concept that means things are the way they should be—our relationship with God, one another, and the world is as it was designed to be. It is a prayer for wholeness, abundance, and integrity.

Go Deeper

Are you longing for a fresh infusion of hope? This psalm looks forward to a time when all things will be made new. We will be in the very presence of God in the New Jerusalem and there will be "no more death or mourning or crying or pain" (Rev. 21:4). Amen. Come, Lord Jesus.

Pray with Us

Today we pray for Your blessing on the modern city of Jerusalem; may Your will be done in the Holy Land. We rejoice in the promise of the New Jerusalem, from which we draw hope! Amen.

BOOK 5

PSALM 123

Lift Up My Eyes

I lift up my eyes to you, to you who sit enthroned in heaven.
PSALM 123:1

It can be easy for our prayer life to devolve into a series of requests: "God can You help me with X . . . ? Can You bring healing to Y . . . ?" And on and on. This is not necessarily a bad thing. Jesus invites us, "Ask and it will be given to you; seek and you will find; knock and the door will be opened to you" (Matt. 7:7). The problem comes when we start envisioning our relationship with God as a customer to vendor or a supervisor to underling.

Psalm 123 reminds us of our proper standing before God. We do not look down on God or view Him as an equal. Instead, the psalmist proclaims, "I lift up my eyes to you, to you who sit enthroned in heaven" (v. 1). God is enthroned over the universe. Our relationship with Him is of servant to master (v. 2). Being a child of God means waiting upon Him, attending His word and obeying. We are at His service.

Being God's servant has benefits. We can expect Him to hear when we call. The psalmist had been ridiculed and mocked by scoffers (v. 4). Because he was God's servant, this was a problem for God as well. Would God allow His servant to be treated poorly? It could be that God had His own purpose for this situation, but this psalm models for us that it is appropriate to ask for God to intervene when we face a difficult situation. We can do this not because God is at our beck and call but because we trust in His mercy and unfailing love (v. 3). We know that He cares. As the author of Hebrews instructs, "Let us then approach God's throne of grace with confidence, so that we may receive mercy and find grace to help us in our time of need" (Heb. 4:16).

Go Deeper
What does this psalm remind you about God? How does understanding our proper relationship to the almighty God affect the way we pray? How does it affect the choices we make today?

Pray with Us
Father, Your Son became the Suffering Servant so that we could be servants to You. Give us desires that align with Your will. Humble and shape us in ever-increasing obedience and Christlike submission. Amen.

BOOK 5

PSALM 124

Seeing God in Suffering

Our help is in the name of the LORD, the Maker of heaven and earth.

PSALM 124:8

It is easy to look out at the ocean, rolling on as far as our eyes can see, or to gaze up at the vast night sky and praise God for His marvelous works. But when we look at the evil in the world and all the suffering and pain, we may question God and wonder what He is doing.

In Psalm 124, the psalmist takes a hard look at suffering and evil and through this is drawn to praise the Lord. The psalm uses two images to describe the suffering the people of Israel experienced. They were almost swallowed alive, and they were almost drowned in a flood (vv. 3–4). Both images draw on our primal fears. Being engulfed by powerful waves with the waters sweeping over us is the stuff of nightmares.

Yet even in this horrific situation, God was at work. The psalmist proclaims that Israel was delivered from certain death, not because of military prowess or diplomatic sorcery. They were delivered because the Lord was with them. God did not prevent them from suffering, but He was with them through it. He also delivered them. The only right response is praise. The psalmist rouses Israel to give credit where credit is due: "If the LORD had not been on our side . . . they would have swallowed us alive" (vv. 2–3).

The God who heard their plea and delivered them is the God who created the heavens and the earth (v. 8). The Maker of the universe cares about us and our suffering. A song of praise celebrating God's power and care might be just the music we need to hear as we face our current trials: "What, then, shall we say in response to these things? If God is for us, who can be against us?" (Rom. 8:31).

Go Deeper

Have you seen God at work during trials in your life? How can God's faithfulness in the past provide you with hope as you face the future?

Pray with Us

God, You are the same One who parted the waves and led Your people through, delivering them safely on the other side. As we walk through the troubles of this world, keep our eyes focused on You, trusting in Your ability to safely deliver us. Amen.

BOOK 5

PSALM 125

Joyfully Secure

As the mountains surround Jerusalem, so the LORD surrounds his people both now and forevermore.

PSALM 125:2

Fear and anxiety are rampant in our world. It is easy to understand why. We are frequently reminded of the fragile nature of our lives, jobs, and the economy. While there are days when life feels precarious, Psalm 125 describes how God's people remained secure and joyful in a world just as uncertain as our own.

If you stand on the Temple Mount in Jerusalem today and look around, you will notice that the city is surrounded by hills. The psalmist sees this geographical feature and draws a spiritual lesson. "As the mountains surround Jerusalem, so the LORD surrounds his people" (v. 2). Those who trust in the Lord have placed their trust in a secure source. As believers today, sometimes we need to be reminded that God cares about us and desires our good. In John 17, Jesus prayed for His disciples, "Holy Father, protect them by the power of your name" (v. 11). In a world riddled by fear, we can be confident in our relationship with God. We can pray with expectation for peace (v. 5).

Our trust in the Lord is not a blind faith or simply wishing for the best. Rather, it is rooted in God's promise that He will one day right all wrongs and implement justice. The psalmist affirms, "The scepter of the wicked will not remain" (v. 3). This psalm models for us how we can both trust that God will one day make all things new and at the same time pray earnestly for that time to come. The apostle John knew better than anyone that Jesus will one day return, yet at the end of Revelation, he prayed, "Amen. Come, Lord Jesus" (Rev. 22:20). Trust, hope, and petition to God go hand in hand.

Go Deeper

What is the source of your security? Your professional or financial success? Your supportive family and friends? How does this psalm challenge those ideas?

Pray with Us

In You alone our hope is found! Remind us, Lord, that You are the only One who can truly satisfy the longing in our heart for safety, for security. When we understand who You are, our only response is to follow and trust. Amen.

BOOK 5

PSALM 126

Filled with Joy

The LORD has done great things for us, and we are filled with joy.

PSALM 126:3

If you were to ask people on the street, "What are Christians like?", what kinds of answers do you think you would get? One of the first things people *should* say about followers of Christ is that they are joyful. This quality is second in the list of the fruit of the Spirit (Gal. 5:22).

Because of their idolatry and sin, Israel had been exiled to Babylon. This must have seemed like the end to many. They had been forcibly relocated to a foreign land thousands of miles away. They had to learn a new language and way of life. It must have seemed that they would never return to the promised land. But God was not through with Israel. After seventy long years, Cyrus issued a decree to allow the people of Israel to return home. Psalm 126 expresses their wonder and joy at this answer to prayer. "Our mouths were filled with laughter, and our tongues with songs of joy" (v. 2).

Joy should be a mark of God's people. Our culture is devoid of joy. We try to manufacture it through endless supplies of entertainment—comedians, action movies, concerts, and bingeable streaming content. But these only provide a momentary sense of escape. Biblical joy is not rooted in circumstances. It does not come through avoiding pain and risk. In fact, this psalm speaks candidly about "sowing with tears" and "weeping" (vv. 5–6). But because of the transformative power of God, those sorrows can lead to joy and abundance. We have joy as we learn to trust that His word is dependable, and His promises are secure.

Sitting in a prison cell, the apostle Paul penned this encouragement: "Rejoice in the Lord always. I will say it again: Rejoice! Let your gentleness be evident to all. The Lord is near" (Phil. 4:4–5). As counterintuitive as it may sound, we can even rejoice in suffering knowing that "those who go out weeping . . . will return with songs of joy, carrying sheaves with them" (v. 6).

Go Deeper

What does joy mean to you? How can the perspective of this psalm change your view of experiencing joy even while suffering?

Pray with Us

"Rejoice in the Lord always. I will say it again: Rejoice!" (Phil. 4:4). Lord, we have joy that the world puzzles at. You bring joy even when the world seems to crash around us. Allow us always, no matter what tomorrow may bring, to experience joy in You. Amen

BOOK 5

PSALM 127

Work and Rest

Unless the LORD *builds the house, the builders labor in vain. Unless the* LORD *watches over the city, the guards stand watch in vain.*

PSALM 127:1

Did you know that we were created to work? While we sometimes grumble about our nine-to-five jobs, God designed work as a good thing. He told the Israelites: "Six days you shall labor and do all your work" (Ex. 20:9). Through work, we feed the hungry, create beautiful pieces of art, disseminate knowledge, construct homes, and create life-sustaining products. However, it is also true that our God-ordained relationship with work has been tainted by sin.

Psalm 127 speaks into our often frantic and restless relationship with work. The psalm opens by reminding us that "unless the LORD builds the house, the builders labor in vain. Unless the LORD watches over the city, the guards stand watch in vain" (v. 1). Notice that the psalmist doesn't say that work is altogether bad. He does not say, "God builds and watches over us, so you might as well go home and relax." The message of the psalm is in the "unless." Unless we recognize that our work is in the context of God's greater work. Unless we remember that our success in everything is dependent upon God. Unless we keep God at the center, our work becomes useless.

It is possible to work hard and achieve nothing of eternal value. Psalm 127 reminds us that we should orient our work toward God. God is at work in the world and has given us the joy and responsibility of joining Him in that work. Children are an example of this. For many of us, our children represent the most significant and lasting impact we will have on the world (vv. 3–5). When our powers of work begin to wane with age, our children will be coming into their prime of life. While our work in their lives may be nearing an end, God created them, and He will continue to work through them.

Every good thing in our life is a gift from God. Today we can build, watch, and labor in trust and hope in what God has done, what He is doing, and what He will do in the world. As Paul reminds us, let's "always give yourselves fully to the work of the Lord, because you know that your labor in the Lord is not in vain" (1 Cor. 15:58).

Go Deeper

Do you ever feel anxious and stressed in your work? Why is that? What would it look like for you to embrace the truth of Psalm 127?

Pray with Us

Our Father, You have given us the gift of work. But we confess that very often we grumble about the work we have to do, whether going to an office or washing the dishes. Help us glorify You in everything we do and thank You for the gifts You have so freely given. Amen.

BOOK 5

PSALM 128

Blessing and Prosperity

Blessed are all who fear the Lord, who walk in obedience to him.
PSALM 128:1

A few years ago, my wife was selected to serve on a jury. She spent a week hearing the sordid details of a particular family. It included specifics of adultery, drug addiction, and deception. Sometimes people think it is difficult to live as a Christian. In some ways that is true. Jesus warned us not to be surprised if the world hates us (John 15:18–19). But it is also hard to live a sinful life. Sin wreaks havoc on relationships, undermines the goals of the sinner, and is detrimental to our overall well-being.

We live in God's world. He designed it and knows how best we should live to navigate it well. The path of wisdom begins with the "fear of the Lord" (v. 1). Fear of the Lord does not mean that we cringe before God. Rather, it describes a sense of awe, humility, wonder, and obedience to the Lord. Proverbs reminds us that "through wisdom your days will be many, and years will be added to your life" (Prov. 9:11). When we live as God intended, it generally leads to a flourishing life. But this truth needs to be understood within the context of living in a fallen world. The results of sin mean that life will not always be for us as God intended. The lament psalms are a powerful testimony to the suffering of the righteous.

On this side of eternity, we experience sorrow, loss, and futility. Even so, grounding our life in the fear of the Lord is the way we were intended to live. Living for God has benefits in the present and certainly in the future.

This psalm reminds us that God desires our good. God blesses us so we can be a blessing to others (1 Peter 3:9). The blessings we experience today remind us of God's promised future for those who love Him.

Go Deeper

What are some ways you have seen sin damage people's lives? What are some benefits of living in the fear of the Lord? What does that look like?

Pray with Us

Keep our lives grounded in You, Lord. Align our hearts and our actions with Your will so that we can enjoy the life that You envisioned for us. And when disappointment comes, remind us that Your promise to us will be perfectly fulfilled in the future! Amen.

BOOK 5

> PSALM 129

Persevering in Pain

"He has cut me free from the cords of the wicked."
PSALM 129:4

When my wife and I celebrated our twentieth anniversary, we looked back on the years and were grateful for the many blessings God allowed us to experience. Things like having children and ministry opportunities. We were also grateful for the trials and difficulties that He brought us through. Both the good and the bad memories gave us reasons to praise God.

When Israel looked back on its history in today's reading, it celebrated not what it had achieved as a nation but what it had survived. From the time of its infancy as slaves in Egypt, Israel had been repeatedly threatened and invaded by foreign powers. The Midianites, Amalekites, Moabites, Edomites, Philistines, and on and on. The list of their oppressors is a long one. In a vivid image, the psalmist compares the violence these nations have done to Israel to a farmer plowing a field (v. 3). Israel had suffered time and time again.

But the Lord had been with Israel even in those difficult times. The psalmist declares, "But the LORD is righteous; he has cut me free from the cords of the wicked" (v. 4). There are many examples in the Old Testament of God delivering and saving Israel. This demonstrates God's righteous character.

The psalm concludes by turning to the present. The psalmist sees those who had turned their back on the Lord. They "hate Zion" (v. 5). This is more than just the disdain of a rural resident for the city. Zion was where God chose to dwell among Israel. These people had abandoned God and were working against what He was doing in the world. The psalmist prays that their efforts would not succeed (vv. 6–8). God would once again come to save.

Go Deeper

How have you seen God work in your own life, both in good times and in difficult times? How does this reassure you that He will be with you in the future?

Pray with Us

Today we pray against the evil at work in the world. Father, foil the designs of Satan, Your foe. Frustrate the efforts of evil people who lead others astray. Thank You for the ultimate futility of the devil's fight. Amen.

BOOK 5

PSALM 130

Hope in Suffering

I wait for the LORD, my whole being waits, and in his word I put my hope.

PSALM 130:5

All human lives are touched by suffering. This is true for Christians as well. Not only do we suffer the normal pains and griefs common to all people, but Jesus promised that we might also suffer because of our allegiance to Him (John 15:18). Jesus did not promise to take our sufferings away in this life. As author George MacDonald put it, "The Son of God suffered unto the death, not that men might not suffer, but that their sufferings might be like His."[40]

Psalm 130 opens with the anguished cry, "Out of the depths I cry to you, LORD" (v. 1). The depths described here by the psalmist are any place that feels desperate. The psalmist does not try to hide his suffering or pretend it is not happening. Instead, he accepts its reality while also embracing the reality of God. In his time of need, he turns to God and asks for mercy (v. 2).

The psalmist recognizes that some suffering is the result of sin. Since all have sinned, God would be justified in allowing suffering to be our primary experience both in this life and the next. But the psalmist knows something else about God. God delights to forgive (v. 4). God made a way for people to be forgiven through the death and resurrection of the Lord Jesus. When this psalm was written, the cross was a future event. However, the sacrificial system pointed to it.

Sometimes when we are suffering, we may wonder, "What can we do?" The psalmist tells us there is something we can do: wait (vv. 5–6). Waiting is not a passive response; it is an expression of hope in God. We wait while recognizing that God is in control.

Go Deeper

Whatever you are waiting for, whatever situation you find yourself in, know that God is on the throne. You can be confident, "for with the LORD is unfailing love and with him is full redemption" (Ps. 130:7).

Pray with Us

Sometimes it takes dismal, desperate times to shake our faith in empty things. Whether we wait in anger, anxiety, or excitement, grow our roots of faith deep in the hope of Your nature and Your promises. Amen.

BOOK 5

> PSALM 131

Content in God

"Can a mother forget the baby at her breast and have no compassion on the child she has borne? Though she may forget, I will not forget you!"
ISAIAH 49:15

The relationship between a parent and child is unique. Parents have authority over their children. In that sense it is like the relationship between a king or a judge and the people. However, there is also a deeply personal element to the parental relationship that makes it quite different. The Bible often uses parental imagery to illustrate the relationship between God and His people. The most common image is of God as a father. In Scripture, God is never called mother. The authors of Scripture are intentional about how they use language, and so we should respect that omission. However, there are places where maternal imagery is used for God.

In Psalm 131, David uses a stunning word picture to describe his relationship with God. He says, "I have calmed and quieted myself, I am like a weaned child with its mother; like a weaned child I am content" (v. 2). Just as an infant finds comfort and security in the arms of its mother, David finds his security in God. Other places in Scripture use this same imagery. Through the prophet Isaiah, God says, "As a mother comforts her child, so will I comfort you" (Isa. 66:13).

This imagery emphasizes that we should have an attitude of humility before God. David confesses, "My heart is not proud, LORD, my eyes are not haughty" (v. 1). He recognizes his utter dependance upon God. In Isaiah, God affirms, "These are the ones who I look on with favor: those who are humble and contrite in spirit, and who tremble at my word" (Isa. 66:2).

This imagery also affirms God's tender care for His children. We can have hope, not because of our ability or efforts to please God, but because of His grace and compassion (v. 3). Like David, we can find comfort and security in the God's arms.

Go Deeper

Describe the relationship between a parent and an infant. How can the picture of God in this psalm provide us with hope and contentment?

Pray with Us

We admit, Lord, that we are utterly dependent on You. You give us life. You feed us. You guide us and teach us. You correct us when we are wrong. You heal us when we are sick. You save us when we are in trouble. You are a good, good parent. Thank You, Lord. Amen.

BOOK 5

PSALM 132

Two Commitments

"May your faithful people sing for joy."
PSALM 132:9

In January 2020, the German government announced that they had created a "help desk" for families who were trying to recover artwork looted by the Nazis during World War II. For many families, the paintings represent an important connection to parents or grandparents who had died in the Holocaust. There was a sense of joy and relief when a long-lost piece of art was returned home.

Psalm 132 tells of two important commitments. The first was David's commitment to return the ark of the covenant back to its central location in Israel's worship. He "swore an oath" and "made a vow" to not rest until this job was completed (vv. 2–5). The ark was not lost. After its capture by the Philistines and subsequent return, it had been residing at Kiriath Jearim (1 Sam. 4–6). The ark of the covenant represented God's presence among His people and needed to be treated with respect. David was eventually successful in bringing the ark into Jerusalem at a temporary dwelling until the temple could be built (2 Sam. 6). This provided a focal place for Israel to worship the Lord.

The second commitment was made by the Lord to David. He promised that a descendant of David would sit on the throne in

Israel "for ever and ever" (Ps. 132:12). He also committed to dwell in Jerusalem and bless it (vv. 13–16). But we should not skip past the "if" statement in verse 12. God expected David's descendants to be faithful to the law. If they disobeyed God, there would be consequences, including exile to Babylon and the destruction of the temple. Even so, God promised that He would ultimately keep His commitment to David (v. 11).

Go Deeper

How does Jesus fulfill God's commitments to David and to us? Consider Romans 1:1–6 and Revelation 20:4–6 as you look at the ways God has fulfilled and will fulfill His promises.

Pray with Us

We may envy those who lived in Israel when Jesus walked the earth, but what a privilege we have to live now, when we can look back and see so many of Your prophecies explicitly fulfilled! The past bolsters our hope for the future. Amen.

BOOK 5

> PSALM 133

Life Together

How good and pleasant it is when God's people live together in unity!
PSALM 133:1

One of the most powerful books about Christian community is Dietrich Bonhoeffer's *Life Together*. Written during the Nazi regime for students in an underground seminary, Bonhoeffer wrote, "The person who loves their dream of community will destroy community, but the person who loves those around them will create community."[41]

Often our dream of what Christian community should be may prevent us from experiencing real community. The reality may not live up to our dreams. Bonhoeffer shifts our focus away from imaginary Christian fellowship, urging us instead to loving the flesh-and-blood people around us.

Psalm 133 celebrates unity within the worshiping community: "How good and pleasant it is when God's people live together in unity!" (v. 1). The word "God's people" literally means "brothers." Anyone who has grown up with brothers or sisters knows that siblings do not always live in unity. From Cain and Abel to the latest church meeting, evidence of brothers and sisters fighting is all around us. Despite this reality, Psalm 133 reminds us of how powerful it is when (with God's help) we live in unity.

The psalm uses two metaphors to celebrate our spiritual unity. First, unity is compared to oil running down a person's head. The imagery here comes from Exodus 29 where instructions were given on how to consecrate priests. Anointing oil represented a time of celebration in the presence of God. When we are unified in God, we are set apart to celebrate and worship Him as one. Second, unity is like the dew on Mount Hermon. This area is well known for its heavy dew, which results in lush and vibrant vegetation. This life-giving image is transferred to the more arid region of Zion. The dew shows us how Christian community brings life and blessing.

Go Deeper

Have you experienced unity within the body of Christ? What things do we do that divide us? What can you do to promote this type of life-giving, refreshing unity among your brothers and sisters in the Lord?

Pray with Us

Father, the older we get, the more we understand the pervasiveness of sin. You exhort us to unity, but how can we love people who, like us, are so flawed? Show us how to love the unlovable and forgive the unforgivable. Amen.

BOOK 5

> PSALM 134

Circle of Blessing

May the LORD bless you from Zion, he who is the Maker of heaven and earth.

PSALM 134:3

For a classroom to run well, everyone needs to do their job. The teacher needs to be prepared, have clear goals, communicate effectively, and have appropriate ways to assess learning. Students need to be attentive, curious, conscientious, and make the most of the opportunity to learn.

In ancient Israel, the priests had a specific role. One of their roles was to represent the people before the Lord in the temple. They would burn incense in the Holy Place and offer Him worship. Psalm 134 has two parts. In the first two verses, the people encouraged the priests to "Praise the LORD, all you servants of the LORD" (v. 1). The word translated by the NIV as "praise" is actually the word "bless," which serves an important role in the psalm. The people called on the priests to fulfill their role faithfully. During festivals, Israel had services in the temple during the night (Isa. 30:29). Even through the night, the priests were to give thanks to the Lord (v. 1).

In the second part of the psalm, the priests respond back to the people, "May the LORD bless you from Zion" (v. 3). The priests were called to "bless" the Lord (vv. 1–2). In turn, they proclaimed the Lord's blessing on the people (v. 3). When the relationship between God and Israel was functioning rightly, there was a beautiful circle of blessing and praise. God is worthy to be worshiped as the "Maker of heaven and earth" (v. 3).

As followers of Jesus, we no longer need priests to stand between God and us. Jesus serves as our perfect high priest and mediator (Heb. 4:14–15). Because of His finished work, we can "approach God's throne of grace with confidence" (Heb. 4:16). We are free to bless the Lord in His presence and receive His blessing. This psalm encourages us as a holy priesthood to offer up praise and thanksgiving to the Lord (2 Peter 2:4–5). There is no more important work for us to do.

Go Deeper

Do you see yourself as a "holy priesthood" called to offer up praise to the Lord (2 Peter 2:4–5)? According to Peter, that is what you are. Let's live into that truth.

Pray with Us

Today, God, we praise You! You have called us into a "holy priesthood" and we offer up our whole selves before you as a sacrifice. Use us. Mold us. Shape us. Forgive us. Bless us. Make our lives a testimony about You before others. We ask these things in Jesus' name. Amen.

BOOK 5

> PSALM 135

Who Do You Worship?

> *Praise the LORD, for the LORD is good; sing praise to his name, for that is pleasant.*
>
> PSALM 135:3

The worship of idols was an important part of life for Israel's neighbors. Skilled craftsmen created idols from the finest materials available. Priests would perform elaborate ceremonies to endow the idol with the presence of the god. The idol would then be treated as royalty. The object would be clothed and "fed" with the best, treated with awe and reverence.

Psalm 135 is a rousing praise psalm to remind Israel that the Lord is greater than the gods of the nations. It was also a stern reminder to Israel that worshiping idols was foolish. These idols were "silver and gold, made by human hands" (v. 15). They had mouths, eyes and ears that did not work (vv. 16–18). These gods could never save or deliver like the Lord. The psalm reminds Israel that the Lord is the One who delivered them from Egypt and brought them into the land of Canaan (vv. 8–12).

Living in the twenty-first century, it is easy to think we are immune to the danger of worshiping idols. But an idol is anything in which we place our allegiance, trust, or hope instead of God. An idol could be our reliance on social media for affirmation or the hope we entrust to politicians. There are hundreds of ways we can fall into the trap of idol worship. An added danger is that we become like what we worship (v. 18).

The good news is that if we worship God, we will grow to become like Him. As Paul explained, "And we all, who with unveiled faces contemplate the Lord's glory, are being transformed into his image with ever-increasing glory" (2 Cor. 3:18).

Go Deeper

How do we prevent idol worship in our own lives? How can praising God turn our hearts away from such things? Today, listen to a praise song that reminds you of God's character.

Pray with Us

We pray with the psalmist today, "I know that the LORD is great, that our Lord is greater than all gods. The LORD does whatever pleases him, in the heavens and on the earth, in the seas and in all their depths" (vv. 5–6). Amen.

PSALM 136

Loved by God

His love endures forever.
PSALM 136:1

When I put my children to bed at night, I remind them that I love them. They already know this. I have told them thousands of times. But the repetition has a purpose. I want them to know that they are loved and that my love for them has not changed.

In today's reading, the psalmist repeats the same line twenty-six times. This could be because the psalm was originally sung antiphonally with a worship leader singing the first line and the congregation the second. But there is more significance to it than that. The repeated line is, "His love endures forever." The word *love* used here communicates "commitment" or "faithfulness." Just as the line repeats again and again, the psalmist is emphasizing that God is not going to give up on His people.

God's unfailing love is celebrated through His amazing works. Sometimes we need to be reminded of what God has done. God is the Creator. He made the sun, moon, and stars (vv. 5–9). When we gaze at the night sky, we are humbled by its immensity and power. But for God it is simply one of the many things He made. In the ancient world, most people believed that the sun, moon, and stars were gods to be worshiped. This hymn reminds Israel that they are objects that God created for His own purpose.

God is our Redeemer. This hymn celebrates God's deliverance of Israel from bondage (vv. 10–15). God's redemption did not stop there. The New Testament proclaims that through Jesus, we have been redeemed from our slavery to sin and death (Rom. 6:17–18). God is our Provider. He loves us by providing our daily bread both physically and spiritually (vv. 23–25).

Go Deeper

Before you finish your devotional time, join with the psalmist in praising God. Sing to Him or thank God for His enduring love. Go forward today knowing that you are loved by God who created, redeemed, and continually provides for you.

Pray with Us

We praise You, the Ruler above all politicians—Your love endures forever. We praise You, the Power over all diseases—Your love endures forever. We praise You, the God beyond time—Your love endures forever. Amen.

BOOK 5

PSALM 137

We Sat and Wept

Do not take revenge, my dear friends, but leave room for God's wrath.
ROMANS 12:19

In 586 BC, the Babylonian army invaded Jerusalem, destroying the city and temple. They took many people captive and forced them into exile. Psalm 137 provides a glimpse of how God's people responded to their situation.

The psalmist opens with a heartbreaking description, "By the rivers of Babylon we sat and wept when we remembered Zion" (v. 1). To make matters worse, their Babylonian captors taunted them by asking them to sing songs that celebrated Jerusalem (v. 3). They were the people who had destroyed the city. It was the kind of request a bully would make to shame someone weaker than them.

The people recognized that they could not bring themselves to sing about Jerusalem, but they did not want to forget the city either (vv. 4–5). They understood that in exile it would probably be easier if they could just forget about Jerusalem and assimilate into Babylonian life. But that would mean turning their back on who they were and on God's promised restoration.

The psalm takes a dark turn in verses 7–9. The people ask God to remember the atrocities that the Edomites and Babylonians did to them and to not let them go unpunished. Israel's exile was due to their own sin and unfaithfulness to the covenant. Still, the Babylonians and Edomites went above and beyond the demands of justice in their behavior toward Israel (Lam. 4:22; Ezek. 35:15; Jer. 50). In this lament, the people vent their anger and frustration to God and beg Him to act. In voicing their disturbing feelings toward their oppressors, they are giving these feelings over to God.

Go Deeper

Are you harboring feelings about injustice? When we walk through difficult times, we can be honest to God in our prayers. One day, God will right all wrongs. Because of Christ's death and resurrection, there is also room for forgiveness and grace even for our enemies.

Pray with Us

Lord, Your ways are higher than our ways. Give us a godly sense of justice and help us see through false, worldly justice. Move us to forgive others, for You have forgiven us so much. Amen.

BOOK 5

PSALM 138

Longing for the Past

I will praise you, Lord, with all my heart.
PSALM 138:1

Often, we do not appreciate what we have until it's gone. As I am writing this, my ankle is in a walking cast. The experience has made me long for the days when I could walk normally, and I look forward to being able to do so soon!

Psalm 138 is written from the perspective of those living outside of Israel. We can be sure that the exiles longed for all that was in their past. They were surrounded by opposing beliefs and cultural practices. But instead of being tempted to give in and worship the gods of foreign lands, David declares, "Before the 'gods' I will sing your praise" (v. 1).

You and I also live in a culture surrounded by other gods, including wealth, influence, pleasure, and power. When we praise God as being the sole object worthy of praise, we are also naming and condemning the idols and idol worship that surrounds us. Only one way is the true way.

Perhaps because of the exposure to other gods, the psalmist has a deepened appreciation for the God of Israel. He recounts what makes our God unique: "Though the Lord is exalted, he looks kindly on the lowly; though lofty, he sees them from afar"

(v. 6). Although God is the Creator of the universe and Lord of all people, He still cares for and sees the humble. God's compassion and faithfulness to His covenant is on full display.

Because of God's greatness, the psalmist prays, "May all the kings of the earth praise you, Lord, when they hear what you have decreed" (v. 4). He desires that people from all the nations will join him in worshiping the God of Israel.

Go Deeper

We can be grateful that we worship the one, true and living God! What "gods" do you see worshiped in our world today? How might our public praise point others to the only true God?

Pray with Us

Heavenly Father, You know us more intimately than we know ourselves. In Scripture we hear again and again that Your love endures forever. Remind us of these truths when we begin to doubt that You will take care of us. Amen.

BOOK 5

PSALM 139

God with Us

Where can I go from your Spirit? Where can I flee from your presence?
PSALM 139:7

This past summer my family and I had the opportunity to visit the famous prison island, Alcatraz. The most severe punishment an inmate could experience there was to be placed in solitary confinement. There is almost nothing worse than to feel completely alone and abandoned.

In Psalm 139, David was threatened by enemies all around (vv. 19–24). In that situation it would be easy to believe that God had abandoned him. To counter this idea, David reminds himself of important truths about God. First, we are fully known by God. God knows what we are doing and thinking. He declares, "Before a word is on my tongue, you, LORD, know it completely" (v. 4).

Second, God is present everywhere. We are never alone. Even if we journey to the farthest corner of the earth or to the deepest part of the sea, "even there your hand will guide me, your right hand will hold me fast" (v. 10). Even in the midst of threatening enemies, God is right there with us.

Third, God cares about us. Before David was born, God was the one who "knit me together in my mother's womb" (v. 13). David's life (and ours!) is under the sovereign care of God (v. 16).

All three of these ideas were countercultural in David's world. Most people believed that the gods were confined to particular places. The gods also did not know everything or care deeply about their worshipers. Some people even thought the gods required child sacrifice. David knew that God is different. He values human life even in the womb (vv. 13–14).

Go Deeper

What types of "gods" do people worship today? What types of beliefs do they hold? How does our knowledge of God differ from their gods?

Pray with Us

Your omnipresence is a comfort to us, Lord—to know that our decisions can never take us outside Your presence; that our sin can never banish You from our lives; that our mistakes can never remove us from Your reach. Amen.

BOOK 5

PSALM 140

God of Justice

Rescue me, Lord, from evildoers; protect me from the violent.
PSALM 140:1

There is almost nothing worse than being falsely accused of a crime or indiscretion. Not only is it difficult to prove your innocence, but your name is tarnished. For many people in this position, their reputation is permanently damaged.

This is the kind of situation David faced. He was confronted by people who used their cunning, intelligence, and social connections to try to bring him down (vv. 1–2). Their attacks against him came in the form of lies: "the poison of vipers is on their lips" (v. 3). Like skillful hunters, they laid traps and snares to catch him (v. 5).

People have not changed much since David's day. They still attack one another with malicious words. In this age of social media, verbal attacks have become common and damaging. What does faithfulness to God look like when we are attacked?

David turned to God in prayer. He vividly described his situation to God knowing that God cared about him and about the truth. He confessed that God was his most secure refuge—"You shield my head in the day of battle" (v. 7). He prayed that his enemies' plans would fail (v. 8). More than that, he prayed that their evil actions would rebound upon them (v. 9).

It is important to note that David is expressing his anger to God but leaves the results in God's hands. His ultimate desire was not for wanton cruelty toward his enemies, but that justice would be done (v. 12).

We can be confident today that every evil ever committed will either be justly forgiven because of Christ's sacrifice, if the perpetrator turns to God in repentance and faith, or justly punished. Nothing escapes God's notice.

Go Deeper

How do you respond to personal attacks? What can we learn from David's reactions to his accusers? How does our faith in Christ affect our reactions to those who oppose us?

Pray with Us

When You created humanity, You said it was very good. Our emotions are part of that good design. May we learn neither to exalt nor deny them, but to accept them as they are, knowing that You remain God in our joy and in our sorrow. Amen.

BOOK 5

PSALM 141

Fixed on You

But my eyes are fixed on you, Sovereign LORD; in you I take refuge.
PSALM 141:8

It can be challenging to be honest with yourself. We tend to give ourselves the benefit of the doubt and assume the best of our own intentions. This is especially true when we face conflict. We are quick to assume that we are right and our opponent is clearly wrong!

In Psalm 141, David turns to God in prayer because his enemies were trying to trap him. But instead of praying immediately against them, David turned his focus inward. He wanted to make sure his heart was right before God. His request focused on three areas. He prayed that God would protect him from saying the wrong thing (v. 3). Words are powerful. They can build people up and tear them down. It is easy to say a damaging word in the heat of conflict. David prayed that God would guard his mouth, that he would only speak words that were right and true.

David also prayed that he would not join the wicked (v. 4). He understood the lure of living for oneself and not for God. He prayed, "Do not let my heart be drawn to what is evil . . . along with those who are evildoers" (v. 4).

Finally, David prayed that he would accept godly correction. "Let a righteous man strike me—that is a kindness; let him rebuke me—that is oil on my head" (v. 5). He knew there would be times when he would need a faithful friend to speak a hard truth. He prayed that he would have an open and receptive heart. A good summary of David's heart toward God in this psalm is found in verse 8, "But my eyes are fixed on you, Sovereign LORD."

Go Deeper
Our words are powerful. Consider how words have been spoken to you that built you up. On the opposite side, how have words been used to hurt you? Ask God to guard your tongue as you speak to others.

Pray with Us
"Set a guard over my mouth, LORD; keep watch over the door of my lips. Do not let my heart be drawn to what is evil so that I take part in wicked deeds" (Ps. 141:3–4). Keep our eyes fixed on You, Lord. Amen.

BOOK 5

PSALM 142

Speak Up!

I cry aloud to the L<small>ORD</small>; I lift up my voice to the L<small>ORD</small> for mercy.
PSALM 142:1

Have you ever been on the receiving end of the silent treatment? One way some people handle conflict is to withdraw and shut down all communication. If this happens with someone you are close to, the silence can be deafening. What makes this even more challenging is that conflict cannot be resolved or addressed until communication resumes.

The Psalms provide many models for us to follow so that we do not give God the silent treatment. No matter what kind of difficulty you are facing, no matter how frustrated you are with God or others, there is language you can use to talk with God about it. In Psalm 142, David is in a cave on the run from Saul (1 Sam. 22:1; 24:1). God had anointed him to be the next king of Israel, but for years he was on the run for his life (1 Sam. 16:1–13). It would be easy for David to be frustrated with God.

In this situation, David refused to give God the silent treatment: "I pour out before him my complaint; before him I tell my trouble" (v. 2). David felt threatened and surrounded by enemies. He lamented, "I have no refuge; no one cares for my life" (v. 4). But in his cry to God, he remembered, "You are my refuge" (v. 5). God is our refuge even when it looks like there is no safe place to turn.

As a follower of Christ, we may face insults or feelings of abandonment by others. The Lord Jesus promised His disciples, "I give them eternal life, and they shall never perish; no one will snatch them out of my hand" (John 10:28). Our future is secure in the hands of Jesus. We can pray in faith with David, "Listen to my cry, for I am in desperate need" (v. 6). We worship a God who is able to turn our laments into songs of praise (v. 7).

Go Deeper

Have you ever been tempted to give God the silent treatment? Know that He cares for you and in His grace has provided us with language in the Psalms to pray to Him even in our sorrows and frustration.

Pray with Us

O God, You see our deepest sorrows. You understand our most crippling pain. We lay ourselves bare before You, God. We cry out to You for help. How good it is that we can feel safe to be our authentic selves in Your presence. Thank You for caring for us so deeply and completely. Amen.

BOOK 5

PSALM 143

Hear My Prayer!

Let the morning bring me word of your unfailing love,
for I have put my trust in you.
PSALM 143:8

From the time of the early church, some psalms were set apart for use during times of repentance and confession of sin. By the fifth century, this group of psalms was known as the "Seven Penitential Psalms." They model how sinful people should approach God. The seventh of these psalms is Psalm 143.

In this poem, David does not confess a specific sin, but he acknowledges his sinful nature. He confesses that "no one living is righteous before you" (v. 2). The apostle Paul used this verse to ground his teaching that all have sinned and fallen short of God's standard (Rom. 3:23; Gal. 2:16).

David realizes that his suffering could be because of God's judgment. He prays for God to deliver him, not because of his righteousness, but because of God's faithfulness (Ps. 143:1). His trust is not in himself, but in God: "I have put my trust in you" (v. 8).

David has good reason to trust in God. He muses, "I remember the days of long ago; I meditate on all your works and consider what your hands have done" (v. 5). He knows the stories of the exodus, of Deborah, and Gideon. Israel did not deserve to be saved, but God heard the prayers of His people.

David's difficult situation made him long for God more than ever. He says that he longs for God like parched ground longs for water (v. 6). He knows he needs God's saving help. He asks that God not only deliver him from his enemies, but that He will teach and guide him in the way he should live (v. 10).

Go Deeper

David models for us how to approach God in humility and faith. Remember today that we are dependent upon God not only for our eternal salvation, but for each breath. Our hope in life and death is that we belong to God.

Pray with Us

Without Your love and forgiveness, where would we be? Left to the unchecked ravages of our own sin, bitter and embittering, lost and hopeless. How deeply and desperately we need You, God! Amen.

BOOK 5

PSALM 144

A New Song

*I will sing a new song to you, my God; on the ten-stringed lyre
I will make music to you.*

PSALM 144:9

Since music started being recorded by tape in the late 1940s, a new technique of musical composition developed that has only become more sophisticated with digital music. Sampling is the reuse of a portion of songs to create something new. It is the foundation of the whole genre of hip hop music.

In Psalm 144, David samples some of his own music. This psalm is composed of elements from Psalms 8, 18, 39, 102, and 104. David does not simply repeat lines from other psalms, he fashions them into a new and unique composition. In the opening verses, David fuses the confident and triumphant tone of Psalm 18 with the pensive musings of Psalm 8. On the one hand God is a refuge and strength for David who enabled him to defeat his enemies (vv. 1–2). Yet, this help makes David wonder, "What are human beings that you care for them, mere mortals that you think of them?" (v. 3). David knows that his life is merely a breath (v. 4). This makes God's tender care for him even more remarkable.

David took these truths about God that he had learned thorough his life and used them as the basis to pray once again for God's help

(vv. 5–8). The tone of this psalm is different. It is more confident in God's provision even in difficulty. This is the song of one who has walked with God for a lifetime and experienced His faithfulness.

This psalm provides us with needed perspective. On the one hand, our lives are fleeting and transient. Yet, God also cares for His people and works for their good. Our significance in life comes from our connection to and worship of the Lord. As David ends this song, "Blessed is the people whose God is the Lord" (v. 15). As followers of Jesus, we know that He has defeated our most significant enemy at the cross. We can rejoice in His victory even as we long for His return (Rev. 19:11–21).

Go Deeper

Can you take different truths you have learned about God over the course of your life and weave them into a prayer of thanksgiving?

Pray with Us

All my life You have been faithful, God. Today, we think back to all that You have done for us. When we consider the many ways You have provided we cannot help but fall to our knees in worship. You are our God! Always and forever! Amen.

BOOK 5

> PSALM 145

Great Is the Lord

The LORD is good to all; he has compassion on all he has made.
PSALM 145:9

Every year different organizations host a Pi competition. In this competition, contestants recite as many digits of the number Pi as they can from memory. The top record holder is Suresh Kumar Sharma who recited 70,030 digits over the course of seventeen hours.[42] The interesting thing about this competition is that no one will ever master it. The number of digits in Pi is infinite. Yet, that does not keep people from trying!

In some ways this has a parallel with Psalm 145. Near the beginning of this praise psalm, David admits that God's greatness is such that "no one can fathom" it (v. 3). It is not possible to fully articulate God's attributes or to describe His nature. Yet, that does not keep David from praise. This psalm praises God from A to Z!

David reminds Israel that praise continues from one generation to the next: "One generation commends your works to another" (v. 4). The next few verses put this into action. The new generation praises God and David responds, "They speak of the glorious splendor of your majesty / and I will meditate on your wonderful works" (v. 5). One of the joys of worshiping in church is when believers of every generation, join in praising God side by side.

David rehearses many of God's attributes. "The LORD is gracious and compassionate, slow to anger and rich in love" (v. 8). He does not tire of recounting what God has done. God is the same yesterday, today, and forever (Heb. 13:8). He is the true king and sovereign over all creation (vv. 1, 13).

Go Deeper
A good exercise today might be to try to write one line of praise to God for each letter of the English alphabet. While we will never fully express the magnitude of God's greatness, it is worth the try.

Pray with Us
You never change, Lord God. You don't lose one attribute and acquire another. And yet to fully describe Your nature would take more breaths than we have to breathe. May the generations forever sing Your praise. Amen.

BOOK 5

PSALM 146

As Long as I Live

*The LORD reigns forever, your God, O Zion,
for all generations. Praise the LORD.*

PSALM 146:10

One of the best-known choral works in the western world is Handel's *Messiah*. Early in its history, a curious custom developed. The audience would stand for the "Hallelujah" chorus, sung at the end of the second movement. Popular tradition holds that this practice originated during the London premier when King George II stood during this song, requiring everyone else to do so as well.

Psalms 146–150 begin and end with the Hebrew phrase "Hallelujah," translated as "Praise the Lord." You might say that these last five psalms are the "Hallelujah" chorus of the Psalter. In today's reading, verses 2–3 demonstrate an important truth. After declaring he will "praise the LORD all my life," the psalmist then warns Israel to "not put your trust in princes." There is a big contrast here between trusting in God, the King of kings, and trusting in earthly rulers.

When we praise God, it helps to center us and remind us where our true hope lies. Our allegiance is not primarily to things of this world. We are people "whose hope is in the LORD their God" (v. 5).

In the second half of the psalm, the psalmist recounts several attributes of God as reasons to praise Him. He reminds us that God cares deeply about the oppressed, the poor, prisoners, the blind, orphans, and widows (vv. 7–9). Not only does this remind us of how compassionate God is, but it also serves as a model for us to follow. If God cares for these vulnerable people, we should as well. Praising God should inspire us to acts of compassion and mercy.

Go Deeper

How can we look to Jesus as a model of compassion? Consider the many ways that the Son of God and Messiah of Israel showed care to the lowly (Luke 4:16–21). How can we follow in His footsteps?

Pray with Us

Time and again, Scripture demonstrates Your concern for the widow, the orphan, and the foreigner. Fill us with Your compassion for the lonely. Give us humility to care for the overlooked with godly love. Amen.

BOOK 5

> PSALM 147

Grateful Praise

How good it is to sing praises to our God,
how pleasant and fitting to praise him!
PSALM 147:1

Almost six hundred years before Jesus was born, the Babylonian army stormed Jerusalem, destroyed the city and temple, and carried off most of the population into exile. By historical standards, this should have been the end of Israel as a nation. In the ancient world, most people believed that if your nation was defeated in battle, so were its gods. It would have been easy for Israel to lose faith. But a generation or two later, the unthinkable happened. They were allowed to return to their land and rebuild their city and temple.

Today's reading is a praise psalm that gives thanks to God for this miraculous restoration. The psalmist declares, "The LORD builds up Jerusalem; he gathers the exiles of Israel" (v. 2). Israel's restoration clearly demonstrated the power of God. God's power is also seen in creation. When you look at the night sky, it is easy to be overwhelmed by the size of the universe and the number of stars. The psalmist proclaims, "He determines the number of the stars; and calls them each by name" (v. 4). Truly His "understanding has no limit" (v. 5). God supplies rain to make grass and wheat grow

(v. 8). He sends snow and ice in the winter, then melts it and brings new life in the spring (vv. 16–18).

Most significantly, God cares about His people. He does not delight in the strongest or most powerful, but in those who trust in Him (vv. 10–11). To be great in God's eyes, one needs only to look to Him as the source of life and salvation. The psalmist rejoices that God has given Israel His word (vv. 19–20). We do not have to wonder what God is like or what He desires. He has clearly revealed Himself to us.

Go Deeper

How do we see the power of God in creation? This psalm calls us to trust in God who created the world, who oversees the weather, who revealed His Word, and who redeemed Israel from captivity. Praise God with the psalmist today!

Pray with Us

Centuries of scientific study have revealed great knowledge of the world, and yet there remains so much we do not know. We worship You, the all-knowing Creator of the universe, from whom no secret can be concealed! Amen.

BOOK 5

> PSALM 148

Praise the Lord!

You are worthy, our Lord and God, to receive glory and honor and power.
REVELATION 4:11

In his book *Reflections on the Psalms*, C. S. Lewis describes why people so naturally praise. "I think we delight to praise what we enjoy because the praise not merely expresses but completes the enjoyment.... The delight is incomplete till it is expressed."[43]

In today's reading, the psalmist is delighted in God and wants everyone to join in the praise. He is not content until the entire universe directs its reverence to God. Twelve times in this poem, the psalmist commands different groups of people or parts of the created world to "praise!"

In verses 1–4, the psalmist looks up and commands the "heavens ... heights ... angels ... heavenly hosts ... sun ... moon ... and stars" to praise the Lord. They should delight to praise God because he created them and sustains them (vv. 5–6). The only appropriate response is to use the existence God gave to point people to Him. The command for the sun, moon, and stars to praise God is especially striking in an ancient context. Most people around Israel worshiped the sun, moon, and stars as gods. The psalmist is clear that they are not gods, but a part of God's created world.

In verses 7–12, the psalmist looks around and calls upon the earth, creatures of the sea, the ocean, storms, mountains, trees, all animals, and all people from king to commoner and from young to old to praise the Lord. As God's creatures they find their fulfillment in ascribing to God His worth.

This psalm should make you feel as if you are a part of a stadium filled to the brim with raucous, ecstatic jubilation celebrating God. God is faithful. He has kept His promises to Israel, His covenant people.

Go Deeper

Praise God! Join the celebration and spend time praising God throughout the day. By yourself or with others, lift your hands and acknowledge that our God reigns. He is Lord of lords and King of kings!

Pray with Us

Praise God from whom all blessings flow; praise Him all creatures here below; praise Him above, ye heavenly host—praise Father, Son, and Holy Ghost! Amen.

BOOK 5

PSALM 149

Fight Song

Let Israel rejoice in their Maker; let the people of Zion be glad in their King.

PSALM 149:2

Many high schools and colleges have a fight song for their sports teams. These songs allow the whole crowd to join in and cheer their team on to victory over their rivals. Psalm 149 is a kind of fight song for Israel, but the battle is much more serious than a good-natured sports rivalry.

The psalm opens with an insistent, rousing, and boisterous call to praise (vv. 1–5). Israel is called to praise God as Creator and King (v. 2). Proclaiming these truths is itself an assault against idolatry. There is only one God who is worthy of our allegiance, the Creator of the heavens and the earth. This God is one who delights to honor the humble and vulnerable (vv. 4–5). Our praise of God should involve our whole being in song and dance (v. 3).

The psalm takes a turn in the second half of the poem. Praise of God leads His people to fight against their enemies (vv. 6–9). Because God cares about the humble and vulnerable, He desires to see justice done. As one commentator put it, "Praise makes war on false gods, false stories, false pride, and false hopes."[44] Through praise, the Lord defeated Moabites and Ammonites (2 Chron. 20:1–23).

This psalm anticipates the final defeat of the wicked at the second coming of the Lord Jesus. Until that day comes, "our struggle is not against flesh and blood, but against the rulers, against the authorities, against the powers of this dark world and against the spiritual forces of evil in the heavenly realms" (Eph. 6:12). We can take up the "sword of the Spirit" to do battle, countering the lies of the evil one with the Word of God (Eph. 6:17).

Psalms like this remind us that we live in a fallen world rife with violence and injustice. It also reminds us that there is a new heavens and new earth to come. We can join the chorus and praise the Lord in anticipation of His final victory (Rev. 19:15).

Go Deeper

Imagine a world in which all rights have been wronged, a world in which there is no sin or sorrow, sickness or death. Let that future that the Lord promised for His children provide you with hope and reasons for praise in the present.

Pray with Us

Victory is Yours, O God! How we praise You for this celebration of Your triumph over evil. Once and for all, Jesus conquered death, so that we can join in this song of victory. We look forward to the new heavens and new earth where evil will forever be erased. Amen.

BOOK 5

PSALM 150

Hallelujah!

Let everything that has breath praise the Lord. Praise the Lord.

PSALM 150:6

My family has a tradition at dinner time. We normally sing the Doxology as a prayer before we eat—"Praise God from whom all blessings flow." This is a special and appropriate way to end each day, praising God and reminding each other of how He provides for us. In a similar way, the book of Psalms ends with a rousing call to praise.

In Psalm 150, the psalmist commands the congregation to "praise the Lord" twelve times! Normally, praise psalms not only call people to praise God, but they also provide reasons to do so. Psalm 150 is unusual in this regard. It does not give any reasons to praise God. Perhaps this is because as the concluding psalm, the psalmist knows that reasons galore have already been provided throughout the Psalter.

We have come a long way since our journey through the Psalter began. We know that life is not always easy. There have been many laments in this book that describe the problem of enemies, sickness, sin, and turmoil. However, throughout the Psalms we see the stabilizing presence of God. He is the one who created us, cares for us, hears our prayer, and works for our salvation.

It is appropriate then to be reminded of all that God has done and will do at the end of this book. In some ways, this ending foreshadows the ending of the Bible in Revelation. After all the trials and tribulations that the people of God will go through, Revelation also ends on a rousing note of praise: "Hallelujah! For the Lord God Almighty reigns. Let us rejoice and be glad and give him glory!" (Rev. 19:6–7).

Go Deeper

As we conclude our study in the Psalms, take time to recount all that God has done for us in Christ. We can look forward to His second coming when all things will be made new. Revelation reminds us, "He who testifies to these things says, 'Yes, I am coming soon.' Amen. Come, Lord Jesus" (Rev. 22:20). Hallelujah indeed!

Pray with Us

God of heaven and earth, and all that is within them—we praise You! We praise You for Your acts of power, we praise You for Your surpassing greatness, we praise You for Your undying faithfulness and love. We praise Your holy name! Amen.